Statesmanship and Soldiership
in World War II

ONE OF FREEDOM'S FINEST HOURS

Statesmanship and Soldiership
in World War II

ONE OF FREEDOM'S FINEST HOURS

Joseph H. Alexander
Stephen E. Ambrose
Thomas H. Conner
Martin Gilbert
Victor Davis Hanson
Frederick W. Kagan
John Lukacs
Herbert Romerstein
Gerhard L. Weinberg

Hillsdale College Press   Hillsdale, Michigan 49242

© 2002 Hillsdale College Press

Published by Hillsdale College Press
33 East College Street, Hillsdale, Michigan 49242
517.437.7341 phone   517.437.3923 fax
www.hillsdale.edu

05   04   03   02   4   3   2   1

Library of Congress Control Number 2002103895

ISBN 0-916308-57-X

Manufactured in the United States of America.

Printed and bound by Edwards Brothers, Ann Arbor, Michigan

Cover illustration "United" by Leslie Darrell Ragan for the War Information
Office, 1943. From the Northwestern University Library World War II Poster
Collection: www.library.northwestern.edu/govpub/collections/wwii-posters

Cover design by Hesseltine & DeMason, Ann Arbor, Michigan

CONTENTS

FOREWORD

The essays in this book are adapted from lectures delivered at a five-day conference held at Hillsdale College on September 9–13, 2001. Their topic is World War II, the greatest military conflict in history. Over three hundred fifty Hillsdale undergraduates attended these lectures and wrote a paper based on them for credit. Over one thousand outside guests traveled to our campus to attend one or more of the presentations. In addition to the historians in this volume, several veterans of World War II took part in the conference, speaking to groups of students at the College and at Hillsdale Academy, the College's model K–12 school. It was a grand event.

A theme began to emerge on the first night of the conference, when Stephen Ambrose argued that the twenty-first century will be the greatest and most peaceful in history because of the victory won by the "greatest generation." Several of the veterans who spoke later picked up this theme. Though they were not so sanguine as Professor Ambrose, they expressed the hope that no one would have to undergo what they themselves endured in the sky above Guadalcanal, crouched behind a sand dune at Omaha Beach, crawling among the sharp rocks at Iwo Jima. But within forty hours after Mr. Ambrose spoke, in the middle of our conference, America was attacked by terrorists and over three thousand of our fellow citizens were killed.

The morning after September 11, at Hillsdale Academy, we heard three speeches by veterans. One was given by Major General Robert Ploger, who, on the morning of June 6, 1944, was a 29-year-old Lieutenant Colonel. He came ashore on Omaha Beach with the job of blowing up a wall, but the explosives arrived some hours after he did, and so he spent a morning under fire, wounded and waiting. His account of that fighting was methodical and riveting.

After the speeches that morning we all went to the Kappa Kappa Gamma sorority house to have lunch. In the middle of the luncheon, Cliff Witte, himself a combat veteran and a brave man, came to me and said that General Ploger had received word the previous evening that his son and daughter-in-law had been killed on the airplane that was hijacked and flown into the Pentagon. The couple had been married only a few days before, and were en route to Hawaii for their honeymoon. General Ploger had spent a sleepless night, unable to travel, unwilling to tell. He got up the next morning and made his presentation, doing his duty without complaint. I had the difficult job of offering condolences at his loss on behalf of the College. When I did so, he broke down immediately.

What must he have been thinking? It is a compound sort of tragedy. We can tell from the statements of the veterans, and from the historians who are close to them, how they take their consolation. None came to Hillsdale to exult in their own glory. Their speeches typically ended with statements like "War is hell" and "I remember so well those who died." Then they would say that they fought in the hope that such fighting would not again be needed. Having instructed the world with great sacrifice in the awfulness of war, perhaps the world would find a better way. Who can blame Professor Ambrose for harboring that same hope? And then, while these veterans were here, our country was attacked and one of them lost a son.

It is a traditional sentiment from many of the greatest Americans, from George Washington to Alexander Hamilton to Abraham

Lincoln, that America is an experiment to be conducted by every generation. It seems that this has not changed.

Those who launched the attack on September 11 did so believing that we Americans are weak and cowardly materialists. Inflamed by hate, driven by demented ambition, they believed that they could use the tools of modern science to destroy the material implements that, they believe, are the sole source of our pleasures and our safety. This is not the first time that such people as these have formed a mistaken impression of us.

In *The Grand Alliance*, Winston Churchill recorded his thoughts upon hearing of Pearl Harbor:

> Silly people . . . might discount the force of the United States. Some said they were soft, others that they would never be united. They would never come to grips. They would never stand bloodletting. Their democracy and system of recurrent elections would paralyze their war effort. They would be just a vague blur on the horizon to friend or foe. Now we should see the weakness of this numerous but remote, wealthy, and talkative people. But I had studied the American Civil War, fought out to the last desperate inch. American blood flowed in my veins. I thought of a remark which Edward Grey had made to me more than thirty years before—that the United States is like "a gigantic boiler. Once the fire is lighted under it, there is no limit to the power it can generate."

It is easy to mistake the love of freedom for lack of virtue. It is easy to mistake the love of peace for cowardice. But these are mistakes, and we twenty-first-century Americans now have before us the hard job of proving so once again.

Political philosopher Leo Strauss once remarked of the contrast between Churchill, "the indomitable and magnanimous statesman," and Hitler, "the insane tyrant," that "this spectacle in its clear simplicity was one of the greatest lessons which men can learn, at any time." Indeed the entirety of World War II is one of those rare events in history whose re-telling will forever guide us toward a deeper understanding of freedom and tyranny; honor and infamy; the roles of prudence, folly, and chance in human affairs; and man's capacity for courage, endurance, and sacrifice.

It is our intention in publishing this book to do our part in preserving these timeless and valuable lessons.

LARRY P. ARNN
President
Hillsdale College

February 2002

ACKNOWLEDGMENTS

Hillsdale College would like to acknowledge the following for their generous support of the conference "One of Freedom's Finest Hours: Statesmanship and Soldiership in WorldWar II" that made this book possible: Castle Rock Foundation, Mrs. Herman A. Dettwiler, Dr. and Mrs. Gordon A. Ewy, F. M. Kirby Foundation, Inc., and Leonette M. & Fred T. Lanners Foundation.

THE LASTING LEGACY OF
WORLD WAR II

STEPHEN E. AMBROSE

I come to sing of America, and of democracy.

We are the first democratic nation-state, and the oldest. Our greatest triumphs are the eighteenth-century creation of our democratic republic, the nineteenth-century abolishment of slavery and holding together of our Union, and our twentieth-century crushing of totalitarianism.

The great legacy of World War II is the throwing of Nazism, the Japanese military, and Italian fascism into the ashcan of history, where they belong. We didn't do it alone, of course. Critical to the victory in 1945 were the other democracies, especially Britain and Canada, and the Soviet Union. But because we won the war, at great sacrifice, we opened the way for democracy to spread around the world. The Soviet Union is gone today, replaced by democracies that are struggling but firmly in place, and the Chinese and Cuban communist systems will soon follow the same path. So ultimately, the legacy of World War II is this: We can worship as we please, live where we want to live, engage in whatever jobs we choose, go as far in our educations as we can, vote, raise our children to know the difference between right and wrong, and pursue happiness.

In the nineteenth century, our best minds labored to discover and describe nature: Lewis and Clark come first to mind. In the twentieth century, our best minds labored to conquer nature: Henry Ford and the Wright brothers, for example, but mostly men like Fermi and Oppenheimer, who invented, developed, and produced better methods to kill more effectively and cheaply. These creators of weapons were engaged in the most critical of all tasks because it was the worst century in the whole history of mankind, with the greatest issue at stake. That issue, simply put, was this: What system could best implement and use the industrial revolution to rule the world—totalitarianism or democracy? In the twenty-first century, thanks to the victory of democracy, our best minds will work on how to restore nature—for example, how to generate electricity and other power sources from renewable resources that don't deplete the earth or create pollution. As a result, the twenty-first century will be the best ever. And it will be so because it was the democracies who won World War II.

On the day the war began, when Nazi Germany invaded Poland, Colonel Dwight Eisenhower, then serving as an aide to General Douglas MacArthur in the Philippines, wrote his younger brother, Milton. He said it scarcely seemed possible "that people that proudly refer to themselves as intelligent could let this situation come about." He blamed Hitler, "a power-drunk egocentric, one of the criminally insane, the absolute ruler of eighty-nine million people." And he made a prophecy: "Hitler should beware the fury of an aroused democracy." It took more than two years for the world's strongest democracy to become aroused, but the Japanese attack at Pearl Harbor united a badly divided American people. Finally aroused, they banded together as never before or since. The most widely used saying in the United States during the war, repeated millions of times, was "We are all in this together." Because of this bonding, America and her allies won the war.

A second great legacy of the victory was the crushing of imperialism. That didn't come about all at once, of course, but it happened because of the war's outcome. Surprisingly, militarist Japan made a contribution to this happy outcome because of its slogan "Asia for the Asians." Still, although the Japanese claimed their aim was to drive the European and American colonial rulers out of Asia, what they substituted was their own rule. Their real aim was to establish the principle that some Asians (meaning the Japanese) would be more equal than others. They drove the British, the Dutch, the French, and the Americans out of their colonies in Asia, only to establish their own empire, which in early 1942 stretched from the Central and South Pacific deep into China, Burma, and elsewhere—the largest empire in history. They ran their colonies in such a way as to make even a Nazi blush. But they were driven out.

The Germans, in 1942, had established their own empire, stretching from the English Channel on the west to as far north as Norway, as far east as Moscow, and as far south as Libya and Egypt. When they were driven back to their prewar boundaries, they were replaced in Central and Eastern Europe by the Soviet Empire. This too failed.

A third legacy of World War II was the atomic bomb. It is possible that had there been no war, there would have been no atomic bomb. Unless its very survival was at risk, no nation would have spent so much money, time and effort on such a risky proposition as making the bomb. And of all the threats to peace and democracy today, the worst is atomic weapons in the hands of madmen.

Still there is a positive side. The making of the bomb showed that there is almost nothing mankind cannot do, especially when a government gets behind the project. Despite the shortcomings that plague every government everywhere, scientific progress is possible with government support. Most of the great projects since 1945 have come about because of that knowledge. Many of them came during the war, including medical advances, radar, jet airplanes, and missiles.

Further, the atomic bomb brought about two great triumphs. First, it forced a Japanese surrender without having to invade the home islands and engage in what would have been the greatest and most costly battle of all, the battle of Tokyo. Second, because the destruction that would result from an exchange of atomic bombs by the United States and the Soviet Union was everywhere understood, the democratic nations won the Cold War without destroying the world. The weapon that brought an end to the Second World War was the weapon that prevented the Third World War.

When he was president of the United States, Eisenhower met with a group of congressmen who urged him to destroy the Soviet menace with an atomic attack, thus eliminating the threat. He replied that he would never do such a thing, then informed the congressmen that despite their desire to reduce or even to eliminate the cost of the Cold War, it should never be done through a first strike with atomic weapons. He went on: "This is a continuous crisis that the United States has to live with. Our most realistic policy is holding the line until the Soviets manage to educate their people." He said that if the Soviets wanted to keep up with the United States, "and they do," they would have to educate their people. "By doing so, they will sow the seeds of destruction of Communism as a virulent power." That seems to me to be an exact description of Mikhail Gorbachev.

America led the way in the destruction of imperialism, not only by doing so much to defeat Japan and Germany, but by repudiating its own imperialism. Even before World War II began in the Pacific, the United States, led by President Franklin Roosevelt, promised independence to the Philippines by July 4, 1946. After driving the Japanese out of the Philippines in 1945, the Americans kept that promise. As a result, democracy flourishes in that country. As a further result of World War II, all the nations of Asia are independent today, and many are democracies or are well on the way to becoming democracies.

America's role in this development includes not only the victory in the war but the example and leadership the United States set in the postwar years. Two examples will suffice: In 1956, when the British and French were attacking Egypt to maintain their control of the

Suez Canal, Eisenhower declared in a campaign speech, "We cannot subscribe to one law for the weak, another law for the strong; one law for those opposing us, another for those allied with us. There can be only one law—or there shall be no peace." A year later, Vice President Richard Nixon, returning from a trip to North Africa, told President Eisenhower that Algeria was not ready for independence. The Algerians would be better ruled by the French, make more progress, than if they ran the country themselves. Eisenhower replied: "The United States could not possibly maintain that freedom—independence—liberty—were necessary to us, but not to others."

Eisenhower was the Supreme Commander of the Allied Expeditionary Force. More than any other democratic military leader, he brought about the victory in Europe. "God, I hate the Germans," he wrote his wife, Mamie. But he never hated the Germans, and one of his first acts as the commander of the American Zone in occupied Germany was to call into his headquarters the members of the German press corps. He told them that Germany had to have a free press if it was to become a democracy. If he did something they disagreed with, he said, he wanted them to criticize him in their newspapers. The reporters were astonished. They had been working for the Nazis for twelve years; here was Germany's conqueror telling them to be critical of him.

Then Eisenhower called in the leaders of the German labor unions and told them that their job was to represent their workers, not the government. They too had been working for the Nazis for twelve years, and they too were astonished. Next he called in the teachers and told them to encourage their students to think for themselves. Again, astonishment. He told his staff that the test of the occupation would be seen in fifty years—that if Germany had a flourishing democracy after that time span, then the occupation could be counted a success.

In 1959, Secretary of State Christian Herter told President Eisenhower that the Christian Democrats in West Germany were afraid of reunification with East Germany—which was the American policy—because they believed that the Socialists in West Germany would combine with the East Germans to defeat the Christian Democrats in a free election. Eisenhower's reply was: "If they get a true free unification, then they have to take their chances on politics." The remark was perfect. It reminds me of something a German student at the University of Munich said to me in 1980: "You Americans sometimes seem to forget, you liberated us too." Any Japanese student could say the same thing.

Nineteen forty-five was the worst year in human history—more people killed, more buildings destroyed, more high explosives, more fires than ever before or since. In 1945, the sight of a group of teenage Germans or Japanese or Red Army troops, in uniform and armed, brought terror to civilians in France, Belgium, Holland, Korea, the Philippines, China, Germany, Poland, and elsewhere. It brought terror because those squads of teen-age soldiers meant rape, pillage, looting, wanton murder, and senseless destruction. There was an exception: a squad of teen-age soldiers of democracy, in uniform and armed—because that squad meant candy, C-rations, cigarettes, and freedom. That was true in France, Belgium, Italy, the Philippines, China, even Germany, and, after August 1945, Japan. We had sent the best of our young men halfway around the world, in both directions, not to conquer, not to destroy, not to rule, but to liberate.

A bright image of the legacy of World War II came from an interview with a veteran. He said that he believed he had done his part in helping to change the twentieth century from one of darkness into one of light. That was exactly right. As of 1945, it was impossible to believe in human progress. World Wars I and II had made a mockery of the nineteenth-century idea of progress—the notion that things were getting better and would continue to do so. In 1945, one had to believe that the final outcome of the scientific and technological revolution that had inspired the idea of progress would be a world destroyed in a nuclear holocaust.

But slowly, surely, the spirit of those GIs handing out candy and helping to bring democracy to their former enemies spread, and today it is democracy, not totalitarianism, that is on the march. Today, one can believe again in progress, as things really are getting better. This is thanks to the GIs, along with the millions of others who helped to liberate Germany and Japan from their evil rulers, and then stood up to Stalin and his successors. That generation has done more to spread freedom and prosperity around the globe than any previous generation.

Sargeant Henry Halstead, who won a Bronze Star, participated in a program after the war that brought together college-age Germans, Frenchmen, and Americans in Munich. The idea was to teach through contact and example. In 1997, Halstead got a Christmas card from a German participant: "I think often of our meetings and mutual ideals. Indeed, the 1948 program and everything connected with it was the most important, decisive event for me. Influenced my life deeply!"

A French participant in the program wrote Halstead: "In 1950 France was in ruins. I saw only a world marked by war, by destruction, by the shadow of war, and by fear. I believed it was not finished, that there would be a next war. I did not think it would be possible to build a life, to have a family. Then came your group of young Americans, attractive, idealistic, optimistic, protected, believing and acting as though anything was possible. It was a transforming experience for me."

That spirit—the spirit that we can do it, we can rebuild Europe and hold back the Red Army and avoid World War III—was the great gift of the New World to the Old World in the twentieth century.

I always ask the veterans I interview to explain why they fought. Some reply with a joke—"for motherhood and apple pie"—and I laugh and fold up the tape recorder. Some ask how on earth I expect them to answer a question like that, and I nod and fold up the recorder. Some give a thoughtful answer. One of the best came from a man who said, "Listen, Steve, I was 18 years old. I had my whole life ahead of me. I had been taught the difference between right and wrong and I didn't want to live in a world in which wrong prevailed. So I fought."

That was why Eisenhower and all his men fought. In a 1942 letter to Colonel William Lee, Eisenhower wrote: "But it is essential that every soldier realizes clearly that the privileged life he has led is under direct threat. His right to speak his own mind, to engage in any profession of his own choosing, to belong to any religious denomination, to live in any locality where he can support himself and his family and to be sure of fair treatment when he might be accused of any crime, all these would disappear if the forces opposing us should through carelessness or over-confidence on our part, succeed in winning this war."

One of those countless GIs who understood what their commander expressed was Lieutenant Thomas Meehan of Easy Company, 506 Parachute Infantry Regiment, 101st Airborne. On May 26, 1944, a week before Operation Overlord, Meehan wrote his wife: "We're fortunate in being Americans. At least we don't step on the underdog. I wonder if that's because there are no 'Americans'—only a stew of immigrants—or if it's because the earth from which we exist has been so kind to us and our forefathers; if it's because the 'American' is the offspring of the logical European who hated oppression and loved freedom beyond life? Those great mountains and the tall timber; the cool deep lakes and broad rivers; the green valleys and white farmhouses; the air, the sea and wind; the plains and great cities; the smell of living—all must be the cause of it. And yet, with all that, we can't get away from the rest."

On June 6, 1944, in Operation Overlord, Lieutenant Meehan was killed. He gave his life so that freedom would prevail.

Eisenhower once said that in war, everything is expendable— even generals' lives—so long as you win. As president, in his Farewell Address to the American people, he spoke to the best instincts of the American spirit: "We pray that peoples of all faiths, all races, all nations, may have their great human needs satisfied; that those now denied opportunity shall come to enjoy it to the full; that all who yearn for freedom may experience its spiritual blessings; that those who have freedom will understand, also, its heavy responsibilities; that all who are insensitive to the needs of others will learn charity; that the scourges of poverty, disease, and ignorance will be made to disappear from the earth, and that, in the goodness of time, all peoples will come to live together in a peace guaranteed by the binding force of mutual respect and love."

That spirit is the legacy of World War II. Because of it, we live today in the richest and freest country the world has ever known.

Notes

The documents cited in this paper are taken from Alfred D. Chandler. Jr., et al., eds., *The Papers of Dwight David Eisenhower* (Baltimore: Johns Hopkins Press, 1970); from the author's two-volume biography, *Eisenhower: Soldier, General of the Army. President Elect* (New York: Simon & Schuster, 1983) and *Eisenhower: The President* (New York: Simon & Schuster, 1984); and from memoirs and letters in the Eisenhower Center at the University of New Orleans.

FRANKLIN D. ROOSEVELT AND THE APPROACH OF WAR, 1937–1941

GERHARD L. WEINBERG

No review of United States policy in the 1930s can make sense unless one begins with the fact that by that time a majority of Americans had come to believe that U.S. entry into the "Great War," as World War I was then called, had been a huge mistake. As the international situation deteriorated in that decade—a process highlighted for the public by Japanese aggression against China, Italian aggression against Ethiopia, and obvious signs of German expansionism in Europe— Congress reflected the people's preference for staying out of what- ever wars might come by enacting a series of so-called "neutrality laws." It is possible that if these laws had been on the books in 1914, the U.S. might not have gone to war with Germany in 1917. But it is as impossible to stay out of a war one has already been in, as it is to win a war one has already lost—though this never keeps some civil- ians in the one case, and some military in the other, from trying.

Although President Franklin D. Roosevelt's assessment of the mistakes made earlier was quite different from that of many others —he thought the U.S. should have entered sooner, demanded un- conditional surrender, and joined in support of the peace settlement— he did sign the neutrality laws passed by Congress, and he did try to keep the country out of war by other policies.

The denunciation of naval limitation treaties by Japan, and their disregard by Germany, led Roosevelt to call for the beginnings of American naval rearmament. This policy was symbolized by the creation of a new class of battleship, the "North Carolina" class, with construction beginning in 1937. This class would be followed by the "South Dakota" and "Iowa" classes in subsequent years. In the diplomatic field, the president had a number of rather nebulous ideas about new international conferences to stabilize the situation, but nothing came of them in the face of Japan's insistence on war in East Asia and Germany's move toward war in Europe.

In view of this, Roosevelt moved in several directions at once. With France clearly weaker than a rearmed Germany, especially in the air, he tried to assist the build-up of the French air force, a process that would serve to increase American aircraft production capacity as well. In November 1938, he also ordered a major build-up of the United States air force. A small program of assistance to Nationalist China in its war against Japan aimed to keep the Japanese busy on the mainland of Asia. In the fields of intelligence and naval planning there were preliminary contacts with Great Britain.

As war in Europe appeared increasingly likely in 1939, Roosevelt attempted two other initiatives that might have deterred Germany from starting another world war. On the domestic side, he tried to persuade Congress to amend the neutrality laws to allow the United States to sell weapons to those who could pay for them and carry them away. Since the sea routes would be dominated by the Western powers, making it known that in case of war those powers could acquire American weapons might induce firmness in London and Paris—and caution in Berlin. Simultaneously, the president urged Josef Stalin, the dictator of the Soviet Union, to align with the Western powers rather than with Germany. Germany, he warned, would concentrate its efforts on defeating France and Great Britain and then turn against the Soviet Union and the United States. If the Soviet Union were aligned with the Western powers, however, the Germans might have second thoughts about starting a war on several fronts. As is well-known, both initiatives failed. The isolationists in Congress were certain there would be no war in Europe and, therefore, no amendments of the Neutrality Act were needed. An equally blind Stalin decided to side with Germany and so encouraged that country to take the plunge into war.

Once Germany began the war in Europe in September 1939, Roosevelt and Stalin followed opposite policies to keep their countries out of war: Stalin helped the Germans as much as possible, while Roosevelt aided the Allies. When the German victory in the West led, exactly as Roosevelt had predicted, to German steps toward war with the United States and the Soviet Union, Roosevelt forwarded a copy of the German plan for attacking the Soviet Union to Stalin. But Stalin dismissed it as a provocation, and continued to provide aid to the Germans until just minutes before they invaded his country.

The dramatic German victories of the spring of 1940 enabled Roosevelt to lead the country in new directions. For the first time in our nation's history, he created something of a coalition government, drawing in the Republican Party's most recent candidate for vice president (after the presidential candidate had refused), as well as the most recent Republican Secretary of State and a number of other prominent Republicans. He persuaded Congress to enact the first peacetime draft in American history so that the country could begin to build an army, even as it began to build a two-ocean navy in the face of threats in both the Atlantic and the Pacific. Far more reluctantly than most have realized, Roosevelt agreed to run for a third term—the only person ever to do so. Against the advice of his military advisors, he believed in 1940 that Britain would hold out and was worth aiding. In 1941, he anticipated that the Soviet Union would hold out and should be aided. Thus there was the possibility that the United States could continue to stay out of the war, by aiding Britain and the Soviet Union to defeat Germany and its ally, Italy.

This possibility became at least theoretically plausible when the British broke the German naval codes, which aided greatly the struggle to get American supplies across the ocean to the Allies. One thing learned from the use of these codes was that convoys of merchant ships could be routed around the lines of German submarines set up in the Atlantic to intercept them. (Far from trying to create incidents in the Atlantic—as some American diplomatic historians still imagine—the British and the Americans used this information to avoid contact as much as possible.) A second fact revealed from intercepted radio messages was that German submarines had been instructed to avoid conflict with the United States. Therefore it was fairly safe to send American ships, escorts, and flying boats through Atlantic waters. As these developments took place in 1941, the U.S. provided the British with a machine that would break the main Japanese diplomatic code, while the British returned the favor by sharing their knowledge of German codes.

The German navy had been calling for war with the United States since October 1939, but Hitler wanted to wait until Germany had either a huge blue-water navy—as he had been planning at least since 1937—or, alternatively, until it could borrow such a navy from Japan, the only other power with a fleet that could challenge America's. It was this policy that, on the one hand, made it possible for the U.S. to send an ever-increasing flow of supplies to Britain—and at least to begin sending supplies to the Soviet Union—while, on the other hand, leaving open the possibility of eventually drawing the U.S. into the war already in progress. That would happen either if the Japanese followed German advice to go to war while the German sun was shining in Europe, or when the Germans had completed the navy they had ordered. They expected to obtain bases for that navy on and off the coast of Northwest Africa, either by diplomacy or by conquest.

The possibility of being drawn into the war, in spite of the aid provided to the Allies, had to be taken into account by President Roosevelt and his advisors. The military forces of the United States had to be built up even as arms left over from World War I, as well as new arms coming out of the factories, were being sent to the Allies. In 1937, the German aircraft industry had been asked to develop a bomber that could fly from Germany to the U.S. and back without refueling. Now the American air force began to work on an intercontinental bomber with a similar ability.

Plans were devised for two different scenarios: the United States fighting by itself and the United States fighting with allies. If the U.S. had to fight by itself, should Britain and the Soviet Union be defeated, those intercontinental bombers would be combined with a huge navy and an enormous army that could land and move to the center of Europe. If there were allies, clearly the most important one would be Britain. Like the Soviet Union, Britain would have no choice but to concentrate first on defeating Germany, even if Japan joined that country in a wider war. Both for that reason and because Germany was the most dangerous of the Axis powers, a "Europe First" strategy made sense for the U.S. if it was to be drawn into war. Although there is no written contemporary evidence on this point, the signs point unmistakably in the direction of Roosevelt's approving this concept—as well as being aware of its general implications.

There remained, nevertheless, a real possibility that the United States could avoid direct participation in the war. The implementation of the Lend–Lease Act, passed in March 1941, followed in June by Germany's invasion of the Soviet Union and that country's steadfastness in the face of invasion, might have allowed the U.S. to assist Britain and the Soviet Union in defeating Germany by themselves. The German victories of 1940 led many in the Japanese government to believe that this was Japan's opportunity to seize the colonies of the defeated nations of Holland and France, as well as those of Britain, which was likely—the Japanese thought—to be defeated by Germany as well. For their part, the U.S. and Britain hoped to stall the Japanese until it became evident that Germany would lose the war. That meant the Americans and the British would have to adopt a procedure that combined deterrence and delay. The deterrence consisted of an American effort to build up armed forces in the Philippines and a British effort to build up forces in Malaya. Delay was created by Roosevelt himself, as he and Secretary of State Cordell Hull invested enormous amounts of time into negotiations with Japan.

Because of the Soviet Union's desperate situation in 1941, the British sent more military equipment and other materiel to the Eastern front in Europe than to Malaya, so that the hope of deterring Japan from attacking southward rested on unprotected large warships. In pursuing this policy, the British government underestimated Japanese fighting ability and overestimated Japanese intelligence.

Japan's challenge to American efforts was of a different sort. In the spring and summer of 1941, the FBI and the Office of Naval Intelligence uncovered the largest Japanese espionage operation in the U.S. Any ensuing public trial of Japanese naval officers who were involved would be certain to arouse the American public against Japan, which would make productive talks impossible. As the Japanese ambassador pointed out, the only way to avoid this was to send the officers home without a trial. After careful consideration, Roosevelt and Hull decided to do exactly that. In a related situation in August 1941, Roosevelt vetoed Operation Marchioness, a combined British–American attempt to sabotage the Japanese ship *Asaka Maru*, which was carrying important materials through the Allied blockade to the Germans. And these consistently pursued delaying tactics came within two weeks of working.

By October 1941 the Japanese leadership had come to the conclusion that the Soviet Union was not about to collapse. They therefore began to urge the Germans to make peace with Stalin, a policy the Japanese would continue to promote unsuccessfully for the remainder of the war. If the Japanese leadership had waited a few more weeks in its rush to war, they would have seen in the German defeats on the Eastern front—first in the South, then before Moscow, and then in the North—together with Britain's simultaneous and successful offensive in North Africa, the possibility that Germany might well lose the war. It made little sense to join the losing side. After all, the purpose of going to war was to seize lands from Japan's allies in the preceding great conflict. But the authorities in Tokyo preferred war to any settlement. When the possibility of returning to the situation of the summer of 1941 was raised in discussions in Washington—whereby Japan would evacuate its forces from southern French Indo-China and the U.S. would sell Japan all the oil it needed—the Japanese negotiators were immediately instructed by Tokyo that under no circumstances were they to pursue such a deal.

When Japan attacked the U.S., Great Britain, and the Netherlands, Germany and Italy—as they had promised—immediately joined in. From the German point of view, it made no difference whether an American warship was sunk in the Atlantic, the Pacific, or the Indian Ocean. Since Hitler knew that the German navy had been straining at the leash, he instructed it to proceed with hostilities following the attack on Pearl Harbor. Hungary, Romania, and Bulgaria also declared war on the United States.

Believing that those nations might be able to go on quite happily without a war with the U.S., Roosevelt insisted on attempting to convince them to withdraw their declarations of war—an effort for which there appears to be no historical precedent. After six months of trying, he gave up and in June 1942 asked Congress to reciprocate. If countries are determined to go to war, there is little alternative, other than surrender, but to oblige them.

It is true that because of the unexpected rapidity of the Japanese advance in the Pacific, and because of the desire of Churchill's government to keep some Australian and New Zealand forces in the Mediterranean theater, more American forces were deployed to the Pacific than to Europe in 1942. However, as soon as possible, the "Europe First" concept was implemented. With the strong backing of his civilian and military advisors, Roosevelt insisted on the earliest possible invasion of northwest Europe. Victory would come by striking at Germany's heart, not by stepping on its toes. To make certain that no third world war would be started by Germany or Japan, they would be forced this time to surrender unconditionally. Although this policy

was not proclaimed publicly until early 1943, there is solid evidence
that it was Roosevelt's and Churchill's agreed-upon aim from the beginning. Thereafter, the U.S. was to play a significant role in the peace
settlement, and the American public was led to accept a continuation
of an international commitment for the duration of the war.

A major role that President Roosevelt played, both before and
after December 1941, was that of bringing and holding the alliance
together. He developed a relationship with Churchill that was close,
but in which each kept his own counsel and his own country's interests in mind. The "destroyers for bases" deal of 1940 exemplifies both
aspects of the relationship. The British needed additional destroyers
for their fight against German submarines; the United States needed
bases to defend the Western hemisphere and to have the capacity to
project American power. The first important meeting of the two leaders, in August 1941, produced the Atlantic Charter, which cemented
their working relationship and led to the appointment of Field Marshal Sir John Dill as the key British representative in Washington. There
he played a central role in the American–British alliance, a fact symbolized today by his equestrian funeral monument in Arlington
National Cemetery.

Roosevelt was one of the few American presidents who had an
interest in and knowledge of Canada, something the Canadian Prime
Minister William Mackenzie King recognized and appreciated. The
president also offered asylum to the exiled royalty of Norway, Holland, and Luxembourg; perhaps he had developed a taste for this
when he had earlier invited the king and queen of England to Hyde
Park. And there can be no doubt that Roosevelt's "Good Neighbor
Policy" toward Latin America contributed to a degree of wartime
cooperation with those countries that would otherwise have been
difficult to imagine.

In his first term as president, Roosevelt had made a major effort
to establish and subsequently to improve relations with the Soviet
Union, but his efforts had not been reciprocated. The Soviet Union's

attack on Finland in the winter of 1939–1940 brought U.S.–Soviet relations to a low point. Roosevelt's description of Stalin's government in February 1940 as "a dictatorship as absolute as any other dictatorship in the world" was greeted by one of the few instances of loud booing during his career. But very much like Churchill, Roosevelt recognized the important role of the Soviet Union, once Germany had forced it to the Allied side. He saw from the start that this relationship would be difficult, but he knew that American aid would assist the immense Soviet war effort and possibly make U.S. participation in the war unnecessary. Alternatively, in the event of such participation, it would enormously relieve the effort the U.S. would have to make—and thus lessen the casualties it would incur.

As president, Roosevelt had another critical leadership role to play: He had to appoint not only America's top civilian officials, but also its key military commanders. In this, Roosevelt had a sure and successful hand. The United States alone, of all the major belligerents in World War II, had the same chief of staff of the Army—George Marshall—and the same chief of the Army Air Force—Henry "Hap" Arnold—throughout the war. Ernest King, the man Roosevelt had called on February 1, 1941, to safeguard the supply route to England, would be the head of the Navy for most of America's participation. Only one theater commander—Joseph Stillwell—was relieved by Roosevelt during the war, and even that was done reluctantly and for unavoidable policy reasons. (It should also be noted that Stillwell was later given another high command position.) As for the army, corps, and division commanders, Roosevelt trusted his chosen theater commanders to manage them. He would review each star and flag rank promotion with great care; but once appointed or designated, the nation's highest officers could count on their commander-in-chief to back them up.

When the Germans invaded Holland, Belgium, Luxembourg, and France in May 1940, Roosevelt asked Army Chief of Staff General George Marshall how many divisions the United States could put into the field. Marshall answered that with some effort, the U.S. could deploy five divisions—and this at a time when Belgium had mobilized eighteen! The build-up of American military power had started late, and while it went faster than our enemies had expected, it still took time. The first of the new battleships, the *North Carolina*, entered service in 1942. The construction of new merchant ships did not exceed losses until the fall of 1943. The Allies did not gain effective control of the skies over Western Europe until February and March of 1944. Few American Army divisions were combat-ready before 1943, and many soldiers fired the new M-1 rifle for the first time when they reached the front.

The slow unfolding of America's military power affected both the military and political aspects of the war. However, what was clear from the beginning was that with Franklin Roosevelt's leadership, the country would harness its human and materiel resources to the attainment of victory. It did so in an alliance that had its frictions and its problems, but that was vastly more cohesive—and better led—than the coalition against which it had been forced to fight.

CHURCHILL'S STATESMANSHIP
1935–1945

MARTIN GILBERT

Winston Churchill's leadership from 1935 to 1945 covers two very distinct phases in Churchill's career. During the first five of those ten years, Churchill was in the political wilderness. During the second five, he was Prime Minister. Yet, these two phases are linked by a single, central, and animating theme: the primacy of national survival and the survival of an open, humane, and free society.

Churchill often described himself as a child of the House of Commons. Parliamentary democracy—essentially the ballot box—and the individual citizen were the focuses which animated his behavior, both in lone opposition and then at the pinnacle of political power. From 1935 to 1939, the society whose survival Churchill so believed in, whose qualities he so believed in, was under threat of malevolent Nazi Germany. Without a shot being fired, democracies in Britain and Europe were under continual threat. During those five years, Churchill, while still a Member of Parliament and able to speak in the House of Commons, was excluded from government. His influence at the center of power, his influence in those places where decisions were made, was nil.

Two successive British Prime Ministers, first Stanley Baldwin and then Neville Chamberlain, believed that an accommodation with

Hitler was both possible and desirable, if necessary, at the expense of small nations. Churchill believed this to be a profound misconception. In Parliament, week after week, he called on the government not to give Hitler the impression of endless compromise, not to neglect the national defense in all its aspects, not to exclude from its policymaking any group in the nation, not to abandon the threatened democracies of Europe, and above all to build up a European front against potential aggression.

In public, Churchill did what he could: He established an Anti-Nazi Council to serve as a focus of debate and of the dissemination of knowledge. To this Council he invited members of all political parties from every strata of British society, from the high aristocracy—that is, from those among them who were not themselves enamored with Hitler— to the trade union movement. He also wrote at least one news-paper article every two weeks describing the nature of Nazism—above all, its racism and its militarism, and the need to be prepared to de-fend against it.

Churchill constantly spoke and wrote about the need for free peoples to be vigilant and active in their own defense; this led to a remarkable phenomenon. Starting in 1934, individuals from the in-ner circles of government came to his home to see him in strictest secrecy to bring him the truth as they had learned it in their profes-sional work, but which the government Ministers whom they served were unwilling to publicize. Hundreds of crucial facts that reached the Baldwin and Chamberlain governments, whether from military attachés or the intelligence services or diplomats overseas—facts that the government would not allow to influence its policy of appease-ment—were brought to Winston Churchill's door.

On one occasion, a British air attaché in Germany had seen secret examples of German air rearmament. On another, a diplomat in the British Embassy in Berlin had heard details of German inten-tions against European countries. On their return from Germany, both went to see Churchill, knowing that their Ministers would dismiss what they reported as alarmist or not in line with British policy. They knew that Churchill would absorb their observations into his speaking and writing, and, above all, into his concept of what ought to be done.

There are many such examples. The government's chief intelligence officer for air raid precaution activity—for every anti-aircraft gun, for every shelter that was being devised—came to see Churchill with the blueprints and locations of these guns and shelters to point out to Churchill that not enough was being done and that the advice of the experts was being ignored. Lord Louis Mountbatten came to see Churchill to show him the way in which the Fleet Air Arm was being run down at the very moment when it needed to be extended. Robert Watson-Watt, the pioneer of radar, was so alarmed by the government's scientific committee refusing to accelerate his work that he asked Churchill to help him.

Why did these civil servants, diplomats, and inventors come in a steady stream to see this man? Because in 1935, 1936, and 1937, Churchill, by reason of his experience in ministerial office and longevity in politics, was one of the most senior figures in Parliament; he had been the political chief or colleague of almost everyone who was then in government. Of course he was able to go and see them: He had instant access. He was able to write to them and they would read his letters. Yet Churchill realized again and again that no matter what the quality of the information he passed on to them, it would not fit in with their desires to come to some arrangement with Germany, and with their hopes that Hitler's regime could be persuaded never to turn its guns and tanks and planes against Britain.

In the secrecy of his Cabinet and of the Cabinet subcommittees which dealt with these matters, Neville Chamberlain confided his belief that he and Hitler could arrange to prevent war between their two countries by agreement and by mutual admiration. He thought they could make plans between them essentially to determine the future of all Europe. Chamberlain went so far as to propose to Hitler an Anglo-German condominium over the raw materials in Africa and the transfer of African territory to Hitler.

Yet, Germany's African territories had been given to Britain after the First World War, as Mandates of the League of Nations, and Chamberlain did not want to dispose of those. He was, after all, not only British but an imperialist. He proposed to Hitler that Britain would retain Germany's African territories, and Germany would be given, as a result of British pressure, large areas of Portuguese Africa. At the end of 1937, the soon-to-be British Foreign Secretary, Lord Halifax, went to Hitler to explain to him Britain's desire for some constructive and positive relationship. He not only found Hitler receptive, but was impressed by Hitler.

Churchill was determined to speak out in the House of Commons against Halifax's visit; Chamberlain tried to prevent this debate from taking place. Lord Halifax contended that the visit to Hitler was private, and should not be the subject of debate because parliamentarians, including Churchill, might criticize Hitler. This would upset the Fuehrer.

Finally, on 12 December 1937, the debate over Lord Halifax's visit to Hitler took place. Churchill went straight to the central point: the racism of Nazi Germany. "That is not a government with which the British democracy can do dealings. It is a horrible thing that a race of people should be attempted to be blotted out of the society in which they have been born. . . . If it were thought that we were making terms for ourselves at the expense either of small nations or of large conceptions which are dear, not only to many nations, but to millions of people in every nation, a knell of despair would resound through many parts of Europe."

Later, when Chamberlain agreed to transfer a substantial swathe of Czech territory to Germany, he argued that the action was legitimate because that area—the Sudetenland—was lived in by German-speaking peoples, despite the fact that they had never been a part of Germany. For his part, Hitler was saying that the Sudetenland was his last demand. In response, Churchill again argued that it is not a question of transfer of territory, but rather a question of morality, and he urged the House of Commons not to ignore "the moral forces involved" in public policy. "For five years I have been asking the House and the government to make armaments—guns, aeroplanes, munitions—but I am quite sure that British armaments alone will never protect us in the times through which we may have to pass." It was a belief in the centrality of moral principles, combined with the fear that Britain was abandoning those moral principles, that were central to Churchill's arguments in opposition, and which were central to his leadership in wartime.

War came for Britain with Hitler's invasion of Poland in September 1939. Two days after that invasion, Britain declared war on Germany. Churchill was brought into the government and put in charge of the Navy—a post he had held at the outbreak of the First World War. Then, in May 1940, he became Prime Minister, and created a truly national government of the sort that Neville Chamberlain had refused to set up, even after the outbreak of war.

The first feature of Churchill's wartime leadership was displayed in a very magnanimous act: He gave full ministerial and cabinet posts and positions of authority throughout the war-making instrument to those who had been his strongest adversaries and critics in the past, as well as to his former supporters. He gave these positions to Right and Left, to Labour and Conservative, to trade unionists and political mavericks, to anyone whom he believed could help the war effort. So lacking was he in vindictiveness that Neville Chamberlain—the man who had kept Churchill out of office in the very years that Churchill believed he could have done something to avert war—remained, at Churchill's suggestion, at 10 Downing Street, because he was a sick man and Churchill did not want him to have the difficulties and inconvenience of moving house at such a time. Thus this man, who had surely thought for many years of the day he would become Prime Minister, did not spend his first weeks as Prime Minister in the Prime Minister's home, but remained in Admiralty House, his former naval headquarters.

Among the Members of Parliament in Churchill's constituency was a young man who, with Neville Chamberlain's encouragement, had tried to remove him from his seat in Parliament in 1938 and 1939. This young man wrote to Churchill on 10 May 1940, apologizing for having, less than a year earlier, tried to eject him from the House of Commons. Churchill thanked him for his letter and his sentiments, adding, "So far as I am concerned, the past is dead."

During the first weeks of Churchill's premiership, many of those who had opposed the appeasement policy of the Chamberlain government were angry that Churchill was not wreaking some sort of vengeance on those who, in the immediate prewar years, had opposed rearmament, and had wanted to trust Hitler and betray Czechoslovakia. In what is arguably his most important speech of the war, the "blood, toil, tears and sweat" speech of 18 June 1940, Churchill broke off from his description of the tremendous dangers then threatening Britain because of the collapse of France, to say as follows:

> There are many who would hold an inquest in the House of Commons on the conduct of the Governments—and of Parliaments, for they are in it, too—during the years which led up to this catastrophe. They seek to indict those who were responsible for the guidance of our affairs. This also would be a foolish and pernicious process. There are too many in it. Let each man search his conscience and search his speeches. I frequently search mine. Of this I am quite sure, that if we open a quarrel between the past and the present, we shall find that we have lost the future. Therefore, I cannot accept the drawing of any distinctions between Members of the present Government. It was formed at a moment of crisis in order to unite all the parties and all sections of opinion. It has received the almost unanimous support of both Houses of Parliament. Its Members are going to stand together, and, subject to the authority of the House of Commons, we are going to govern the coun-

try and fight the war. It is absolutely necessary at a time like this that every Minister who tries each day to do his duty shall be respected, and their subordinates must know that their chiefs are not threatened men, men who are here to-day and gone to-morrow, but that their directions must be punctually and faithfully obeyed. Without this concentrated power we cannot face what lies before us.

So he insisted on absolute loyalty within his government toward those who had been, just a few months earlier, his strongest critics.

Following his own advice, Churchill appointed, as Secretary of State for War, David Margesson, who as Chief Whip had organized Parliament in such a way as to make debate difficult, thereby ensuring that Churchill would have less opportunity to speak. Churchill knew that Margesson, a soldier in the First World War and a man of considerable bravery, would make a first class Secretary of State for War.

A second factor in Churchill's leadership—and this had been seen during his wilderness years—was his ability to speak to ordinary people. He had no edge to his voice. Although he came from a very aristocratic family, he had no aristocratic airs. His great delight— if he found himself in a street with a group of people who had been badly bombed, or a street in which soldiers were parading, or where firefighters were getting ready for the evening's blitz and subsequent burning—was to stride forward from his aides and assistants and from his guard like a schoolboy into the midst of a melee. He was quite a small person, and would disappear, surrounded by the people with whom he wanted to speak. The British public recognized his great quality in this regard. Someone once asked Churchill, "Why is it called the century of the common man?" (This was a phrase that people commonly used about the twentieth century.) He replied, "It is called the century of the common man because, in it, the common man has suffered most." The man and woman in the street in Britain knew that he understood their plight.

The third feature of Churchill's leadership—his ability to convince those around him that victory was possible, even in the darkest hours—is something very difficult to reconstruct today because we know that the war was won by the Allies, and that Hitler and Nazism were destroyed. Germany's unconditional surrender in 1945 meant that what was probably the most important single aim of Churchill and Roosevelt together—victory—was achieved. But in May and June of 1940, free people were not pondering the defeat of Germany, but whether Britain herself could survive through that summer and autumn and into the winter.

A curious fact—one of many with which the rich tapestry of history is woven—is that when Churchill spoke in the House of Commons, he did not contemplate his remarks being broadcast. It was Neville Chamberlain, whom Churchill had kept in his government, who said at a Cabinet meeting that it would be important for British morale that Churchill broadcast to the British people. Following Chamberlain's suggestion, Churchill gave his first broadcast as Prime Minister, and what he said holds the key to the success of his leadership. He spoke at some length about immediate dangers, but then he turned to an unexpected topic:

> You ask, what is our aim? I can answer in one word: Victory —victory at all costs, victory in spite of all terror, victory however long and hard the road may be; for without victory, there is no survival. Let that be realized; no survival for the British Empire; no survival for all that the British Empire has stood for; no survival for the urge and impulse of the ages, that mankind will move forward towards its goal. But I take up my task with buoyancy and hope. I feel sure that our cause will not be suffered to fail among men.

To talk of victory in the midst of the Blitz, and to link that victory with the progress of mankind, was something extraordinary and it caught the people's imagination. If this man, who surely knew all of the facts of the situation, and especially the bad ones, could still use the word victory and make victory his aim, then there was a reason, not just to hold on, but to work even harder for that victory.

These aspects of Churchill's leadership reflected the many facets of his character and of his experience—an experience that, in 1940, went back forty years. He had experienced warfare at the end of the nineteenth and beginning of the twentieth centuries, and also during the First World War, in the trenches on the Western Front. He had no illusions about what war meant, writing once to his wife of war's "vile and utter folly and barbarism." He knew war could be horrendous, but as he explained to the House of Commons after Neville Chamberlain had expressed support for ceding Czech territory to Hitler, "War is terrible, but slavery is worse."

The British people did not want to be slaves. Dictatorship and totalitarianism were as alien to them as foreign rule, and they had confidence that Churchill shared this view because he had expressed it all his life. He had labored day and night during the First World War on several tasks of central importance to the achievement of victory, including long, hard hours in 1917 and 1918 as Minister of Munitions. Churchill's experiences between the wars had also brought him to a clear understanding of how easy it was for democracy to be overwhelmed, whether by Communism in Russia in 1917 or by Nazism in Germany in 1933. He had watched with horror the Japanese invasion, pillage, and destruction in China in 1937, and the destruction of Ethiopia, using poison gas, by Mussolini's Italy.

It is surprising how often this man—a man described by some historians as grumpy, moody, grim looking, frowning, almost tyrannical, and even a depressed drunk—was a source of enlightenment and encouragement to those around him. Generals would come to see him wondering whether they were going to get a flea in the ear, and would find that he had not only studied their actions very carefully, but would approve their actions and urge them on. On one occasion in April 1941, a very nervous British diplomat, who was doing important work in Belgrade attempting to bring about a pro-Allied revolution among the pro-German administration, sent Churchill a telegram describing what he had done and asking how he should proceed. The encouraging reply: "Continue to pester, nag, and bite"— which the diplomat certainly did.

Churchill would accept responsibility for difficult decisions as a way to encourage—and also to protect—those serving under him. Probably the single most difficult wartime decision he had to make was whether to bombard the French fleet at Oran. The French admiral there had refused to hand over his section of the French fleet to the British, and had also refused to sail his ships to a neutral port or to the Caribbean. Britain was on the verge of being invaded by Germany, which would almost certainly commandeer those French warships and use them as part of the German invasion fleet. The decision to bombard the French vessels while at anchor would surely result in the deaths of Frenchmen who had been Britain's allies only a few weeks before. All Admiralty orders to the fleet were signed by the First Sea Lord, who in this case was Admiral Pound. To Pound, then, fell the duty to actually send the order to bombard the French fleet. But before he could do so, Churchill offered to sign the order himself, not wanting this professional sailor to be tarnished by a decision which Churchill knew would be a matter of deep historical controversy in subsequent years.

Churchill would also anguish over the decision to remove army commanders, men who were often popular with the British people, such as Generals Wavell and Auchinleck. Yet, when he received staff reports describing a commander's exhaustion and inability to carry out his duties effectively, Churchill had no choice but to act. Although he received the brunt of public opprobrium for having sacked a commander, he stood firm, determined to have the commanders-in-chief whom he regarded as best able to do the job. One such general was Bernard Montgomery, whose appointment was met with skepticism from many quarters, including from Churchill's wife, Clementine, who wrote to him of how she had heard that Montgomery was somewhat disagreeable. Churchill replied, "If he is disagreeable to those about him, he is also disagreeable to the enemy." And so it proved.

Churchill's leadership benefited from two factors: The first was what the British call the Private Office, or the private secretariat at 10 Downing Street. Five young men—in their late twenties and early thirties—were with Churchill day and night in alternating teams, and hour after hour brought to him locked boxes filled with letters, problems, and requests. These young men had to know what to put in front of him and how much to put in front of him. A document at the top of the box represented a situation or a problem that required immediate attention by the Prime Minister. During the course of an evening, five or six boxes would be brought up—or even more at times of crisis—and as the problems presented in one of them were dealt with, another one would take its place. On one occasion, when one of the typing ladies to whom he dictated his responses to the material in the boxes began to grow weary, Churchill looked at her with his beatific smile and said, "My dear, we must all go on, like the gun horses, till we drop." (In the First World War, it was the gun horses who pulled the artillery limbers.)

Because of the incredible pressures on his time, Churchill, along with his Private Office, developed an amazing system of delegation of work. This system of delegation included several important committees of experts. Once Churchill had given general instructions about what needed to be done, those committees worked uninterrupted by him. Each committee would then submit its proposals, which would usually receive the initials "WSC" in the margin as a sign of Churchill's approval. When he did not approve, he could then respond with an entire essay. At the center of this delegation during the crisis months of 1940 was the Defence Committee of the War Cabinet, of which Churchill was the Chairman. The Committee often met twice a day, usually deciding on two or three major issues relating to the conduct of the war—the dispatch of troops, the bombing offensives, the relationship with the United States, which military operations to approve, which to postpone, which to review. No one had a dictatorial say in this committee. If Churchill wanted something, however strongly, and three of the other five members were opposed to it, he did not go ahead. Churchill was not shy or timid—when he made his case he could do so with great emphasis—but if the Defence Committee opposed it, it did not happen. The committee, however, was not a contest over who spoke the loudest. It was a desperate attempt to find the right answer to daily questions of vital importance to the conduct of the war.

Churchill's greatest quality of leadership in the Second World War—a quality often mischaracterized by some of his biographers as "interference"—was his ability to watch every aspect of the war like a hawk. For example, Churchill understood from the first day of his premiership that without American participation, support, help, and eventual direct involvement, there could be no victory. He also understood the existence of anti-American sentiment penetrating British society, including official circles. He insisted on seeing every telegram from every British mission in Washington, and he would search for anything he thought was belittling to the United States. One result of this was that a distinguished Admiral, who thought he knew far better than the United States how the war should be conducted, was recalled from the United States—with Churchill issuing a statement that he would not allow expressions of anti-Americanism by Britain's representatives in Washington.

Churchill's hawklike vigilance extended to the ships crossing between America and Britain—ships about which his photographic memory enabled him to know almost every detail regarding their cargo, their speed, to what convoy, if any, they belonged, where they loaded and unloaded, and for how long. If something seemed remiss, he would act to secure a remedy. This was not a man who sat inactive while the war raged, but rather one who did his best to know all he could about it, for the sake of the ultimate goal of victory. Criticized on one occasion in Parliament for not being active enough, Churchill replied, "I certainly do not think I am one of those who needs to be prodded. In fact, if anything, I am a prod."

The majority of Churchill's parliamentary speeches were long (they could run to two hours) and very detailed. He was the master of expounding a complicated case in considerable detail. Churchill believed that it was important to lead his critics through each point of his argument, step-by-step, without shortcuts. By 1940, Churchill had forty-five years of experience of addressing audiences. He had travelled from city to city since the 1890s, talking to people and expounding his views and policies. He knew how to communicate.

One story illustrates his abilities in this regard very well. After the fall of France in 1940, Churchill decided to broadcast a speech to the French people. He prepared, in English and in French, a short message which conveyed the lesson that bad times had come, but eventually things would be all right. He was a great student of French history, and in the course of this speech he wanted to refer to a remark Napoleon had made on the eve of the Battle of Waterloo, which he thought would give the French a tremendous boost in morale. Napoleon had said, "These same Prussians, who are so boastful today, were three to one at Jena, and six to one at Montmirail." But just as Churchill was about to say, "Remember how Napoleon said before the Battle of Waterloo," he suddenly realized that he could not talk to the French—in October 1940—about the Battle of Waterloo, which they had lost, and he substituted, spontaneously, the phrase, "As Napoleon said before one of his battles...."

Leadership has to combine long-term planning and instantaneous responses.

Note

The documents cited in this paper are take from Volumes Five, Six, and Seven of the author's official biography of Sir Winston Churchill; and from the document volumes *The Churchill War Papers*, Volumes 1, 2, and 3.

D-DAY: HOW TO READ A BATTLE

THOMAS H. CONNER

My interest in World War II, and in the story of D-Day, is not so much professional as it is personal—rooted in family experiences and, later in life, in my own travels to the battle sites in Europe. I grew up around a dinner table during the 1950s at which the war was a frequent topic of conversation. My father had spent two years in the Army, although he never saw combat. Every time my mother re-lived his departure for military service in February 1944, she recalled that as he walked across the backyard and shut the gate behind him, she never expected to see him again. He was drafted at a time when everyone on both sides of the Atlantic fully expected the long-awaited invasion of northwestern Europe to take place, and my mother assumed that my father was headed abroad for the decisive battle against Hitler. It didn't turn out that way for him, but it did for countless others. Every time I heard those stories as a youngster, I was impressed by the magnitude of what was being discussed. I couldn't grasp details, but I could grasp the enormity.

For anyone who was alive during World War II, I suspect it is safe to say that the war was the major event of their lives. John Keegan, in fact, wrote some years back that World War II was "the largest single event in human history."[1] It could be, too, that June 6, 1944, was the most significant single day in that long, tortuous struggle. The code-name Overlord that was given to the attack on Normandy indicates how the planners understood its importance to the outcome of the war. Certainly historians have never spared superlatives when writing about D-Day. In this, they are merely taking their cue from the participants in the event.

"There were many D-days in World War II," wrote Forrest Pogue, the biographer of General George C. Marshall, "but only one is understood when the term is mentioned. For the Western powers, at least, it represented the final focus of efforts to win a definite victory over the Axis in Europe."[2] Carlo d'Este, author of one of the best monographs on the Battle of Normandy, called it "the most complex and daring military operation in the history of modern warfare."[3] "The most decisive assault of the war," wrote General Omar Bradley in his memoirs.[4] "Much the greatest thing we have ever attempted," a worried Winston Churchill remarked early in the planning stages.[5] *D-Day, June 6, 1944: The Climactic Battle of World War II* proclaims the title of one of Stephen Ambrose's books.[6]

The Germans seemed inclined to agree with all of these characterizations, but especially the latter. Hitler himself declared, in November 1943, that the decisive battle for Germany would be fought on the French coast. Ten weeks before the Allies attacked, the Fuehrer told his generals: "The destruction of the enemy's landing attempt means more than a purely local decision on the Western Front. It is the sole decisive factor in the whole conduct of the war and hence in its final result. . . . [T]he whole outcome of the war depends on each man fighting in the West, and that means the fate of the Reich as well."[7] It is worth remembering that the first person to assign the term "the longest day" to the events of June 6, 1944, was not the author Cornelius Ryan, but rather General Erwin Rommel, who, as he looked forward to the inevitable moment six weeks before it came, remarked to an aide:

> Believe me, Lang, the first twenty-four hours of the invasion will be decisive. . . . [T]he fate of Germany depends

on the outcome. . . . [F]or the Allies, as well as Germany, it
will be the longest day. [8]

It might be said, too, that "the longest day" was a long time
coming. D-Day occurred 1,463 days after the last British troops were
evacuated from Dunkirk in June 1940. Winston Churchill had pre-
sided over that debacle, masked as a miracle, during his first month
as prime minister. Within a matter of months the indomitable British
leader was encouraging BBC listeners in occupied France to hope for
"the morning":

> Good night, then: sleep to gather strength for the morn-
> ing. For the morning will come. Brightly will it shine on
> the brave and the true, kindly upon all who suffer for the
> cause, glorious upon the tombs of heroes. Thus, will shine
> the dawn.[9]

This was in October 1940. Britain was standing alone against the conqueror, the recently defeated French were openly avowing their intention to collaborate with the Germans in building a "new European
order," and the Nazi–Soviet alliance was solidly in place. Meanwhile,
freedom's great hope on the other side of the Atlantic seemed firm in
its belief that the ocean was an invincible shield against any designs
the gangsters in Berlin might have on it.

By the beginning of 1942, however, much had changed. The
Americans were in the war; the Anglo–American leadership had
agreed on a "Europe-First" strategy; and the Russians, now dangerously beleaguered as Hitler's enemy, were clamoring for a "Second
Front," by which they meant the reopening of the Western Front that
had gone quiet in June 1940. The Americans were most eager to oblige
their new allies, and at mid-year, President Roosevelt promised Stalin a new front in Europe by the end of 1942—long before the U.S.
was capable of delivering it successfully. (It should be emphasized
that this was not the best medicine for the suspicion of the "capitalist

and imperialist" Allies that haunted the Kremlin.) Failing that, the Americans produced Operation Torch—the invasion of North Africa. And 1943 brought invasions of Sicily and Italy.

With all due respect to what these actions gained, they were sideshows in comparison to *the* Second Front. No one sensed this more keenly than Stalin, but the thought nagged at the Americans too. As the first two years of U.S. participation in the war against Germany drew to a close, the growing conviction on this side of the Atlantic was that Hitler would not be defeated until an army had crossed the Channel and driven across the Rhine. The British were not altogether averse to this thinking, and eventually signed on fully with Overlord. But as late as April 1944, Churchill was complaining that the operation had been "forced upon us by the Russians and by the United States military authorities." It was only on May 15, 1944, at the final review of the invasion plans, that he conceded he was "hardening toward this enterprise."[10]

Perspectives on reopening the Western Front were different within the Anglo–American camp, largely as a result of Britain's experience in World War I, when fighting in France had meant static and terribly bloody trench warfare. The Americans had been in combat in World War I also, but only in the final six to eight months of a contest that had lasted more than four years; U.S. casualties had been barely ten percent of what the British had suffered. Keeping this in mind makes it easier to understand why Churchill was inclined to pursue victory in World War II by other means if possible.

A key step was taken in December 1943, when Roosevelt and Churchill decided upon the command structure for the invasion. The top command position went to General Dwight Eisenhower, while General Montgomery was to lead the ground forces in the assault.[11] The naval and air contingents were given to British officers Sir Bertram Ramsey and Sir Trafford Leigh-Mallory, respectively. Once named, General Eisenhower took up headquarters in London, where planning had been underway for some time under the direction of British General Frederick Morgan. The original plan called for three infantry divisions to land on the beaches, with airborne divisions in support on the flanks. Both Eisenhower and Montgomery agreed that the assault force needed to be larger, and on D-Day five entire infantry divisions, some of them reinforced by parts of other divisions, invaded from the sea, supported by three airborne divisions, for a total of almost 156,000 men on the ground. Eleven thousand aircraft and five thousand ships transported and supported this force. The extra strength, in turn, required more landing craft and logistical support of various sorts, so the original May target date was put back to early June. Because the planners wanted the right mix of moonlight (to aid the paratroopers) and low tides at daybreak (to expose the German beach obstacles), only two clusters of days in June were deemed suitable: June 5, 6, or 7, and then again about two weeks later.

Of the hundreds of miles of German-occupied coastline to choose from, why did the Allies identify the beaches of Normandy as the most desirable landing sites? First, these areas were less than a day's sail from southern England, and also within range of fighter cover from English bases. Second, their topography was suited to the movement of large numbers of men and motorized equipment. Third, and perhaps most critically, they were far enough from major ports that the Germans would not have unduly formidable defenses there, but close enough to ports to make likely the capture of a port within a short time of the invasion. Hitler's much trumpeted "Atlantic Wall" was not a continuous line of fortifications, but was strongest around the major ports—especially at Pas-de-Calais, the shortest step across the Channel, and at other ports such as Dunkirk. From the Dieppe raid in August 1942, the Germans had drawn the lesson that if the Allies ever did try to cross the Channel in force, they would likely do so at a port, because such facilities would be necessary to keep the troops supplied and reinforced. "Hold the ports, and we hold Europe" fairly well summarizes the German strategy for defending against amphibious assault. The Allies, who had been stung severely at Dieppe, had taken precisely the opposite lesson from the experience—

namely, that attacking a port would probably spell disaster.[12] Cherbourg (at the tip of the Cotentin peninsula) and LeHavre (in the Seine estuary) are within roughly thirty miles of the Normandy landing area, but still well removed from it. This was all important. Artificial harbors—so the Allied planners reasoned but the Germans never guessed—would fill the logistical bill until such time as an established port could be seized.[13]

Getting a force to France that was large enough and strong enough to seize a substantial beachhead from an enemy that was far more numerous in the overall theater was one thing. But the Allied strategy for success on D-Day included at least three additional elements designed to frustrate the enemy's ability to bring its numerical advantage to bear against the point of attack. One of these elements was a massive campaign of bombing from the air and sabotage from the ground aimed at the transportation system of France. For two months before D-Day, Allied bombers ranged the full length of the French coast and well inland, destroying railways and highways that might be used to supply German reinforcements and taking a heavy toll on French civilians. Additionally, just prior to the landings, the French resistance carried out local sabotage missions aimed at further crippling German communications. The second element was a launch by the Soviets of a major summer offensive in 1944, which kept the Germans from relocating large units to the West. And third there was an intricate deception—Operation Bodyguard, more commonly referred to as Operation Fortitude—which successfully convinced the Germans that a follow-up to the landing on Normandy was aimed at the Pas-de-Calais.[14]

This deception, which played a significant part in Overlord's success, consisted of an effort by British counterintelligence to turn German spies and to have them feed misinformation to Berlin; of fictitious radio traffic surrounding fictitious armies aimed at the narrowest part of the Channel; and even of recorded sounds of tank traffic played over loudspeakers, in what would have been the likeliest staging areas for an attack on Calais. That General George S. Patton, Jr., whom the Germans greatly admired, was the head of this phony invasion force was an added, and apparently effective, part of the trick. The deception kept an entire German army group frozen in northeastern France until early August, by which time the Allies had broken out of the Normandy beachhead for good.

That German reinforcements, especially the all-important armored divisions closer to Normandy, never made a concerted effort to counterattack the beachheads was Hitler's fault. He required his Western commanders first to clear directly with Berlin the deployment of their units to meet a perceived Allied invasion. Even when some Panzer divisions were released for the fight in Normandy, they tended to dribble in piecemeal, or else they were so harassed by Allied air raids and the transportation tangle that they were ineffective.

The genius of Allied planning and the faults of the German response played their important, even crucial, parts in the success of D-Day. Intangibles—such as the remarkable capacity of American soldiers to overcome unforeseen developments, which Stephen Ambrose emphasizes in his books and credits to the atmosphere of freedom in which these young men grew up—played their roles, too. Lady luck smiled on Overlord in a host of ways as well, most notably with the weather. It is well-known that the operation had to be postponed twenty-four hours from its scheduled date of June 5 because of storm conditions in the Channel. However, the meteorologists picked up on a break in the bad weather for June 6, which permitted General Eisenhower, after agonizing reflection, to give the go-ahead for the next day. The Germans, as it turned out, had no capacity to forecast the weather; their weather planes had been cleared from the sky, along with the rest of their air power. Thus, for all the Germans knew, the storm was going to last and would keep the Allies from coming ashore anytime soon.[15] This caused them to let their guard down on June 6. General Rommel, who had done so much to prepare his forces for this day, was not even in France, having taken leave to return to Germany for his wife's fiftieth birthday. By the time he whisked himself back to his headquarters later that day, his opportunity to stop the Allies on the beaches was lost.

General Eisenhower's exhortation to the troops of D-Day began as follows:

> Soldiers, Sailors, and Airmen of the Allied Expeditionary Force! You are about to embark upon the Great Crusade, toward which we have striven these many months. The eyes of the world are upon you. The hopes and prayers of liberty-loving people everywhere march with you. In company with our brave Allies and brothers-in-arms on other Fronts, you will bring about the destruction of the German war machine, the elimination of Nazi tyranny over the oppressed peoples of Europe, and security for ourselves in a free world.[16]

These words capture the great sense of anticipation that had been building throughout the world as this moment approached, and speak to how the Allies understood the stakes. The object of D-Day was to begin the final destruction of the German war machine and restore liberty to those who had endured the Nazi yoke since the early campaigns in Europe. Once that object was fulfilled, it was hoped, the world would be secure for all who loved freedom. The General went on to acknowledge that the task of victory "will not be an easy one. Your enemy is well-trained, well-equipped, and battle-hardened. He will fight savagely." But Eisenhower explained that the Germans had been greatly weakened by a string of defeats since 1941. "The tide has turned!" he exclaimed. "The free men of the world are marching together to Victory!" He concluded with a plea for "us all [to] beseech the blessing of Almighty God on this great and noble undertaking."[17]

Behind the confidence expressed in public lay genuine anxiety about the prospects for Overlord's success. Admiral Ramsey confided to his diary on June 5: "I am not under delusions as to the risks involved in this most difficult of all operations. . . . We shall require all the help that God can give us. . . ."[18] After attending his first Overlord briefing, U.S. Admiral Morton Deyo remarked, "It seemed to us that the proper meshing of so many gears would need nothing less than divine guidance."[19] Alone in his trailer at midday on June 5, Eisenhower penned a press statement to be issued in the event that Overlord did not succeed:

> Our landings . . . have failed and I have withdrawn the troops. My decision to attack at this time and place was based upon the best information available. The troops, the air and the Navy did all that bravery and devotion to duty could do. If any blame or fault attaches to the attempt it is mine alone.[20]

These words are notable not only for what they reveal of Eisenhower's appreciation of the risks, but for what they tell us of his character.

Stephen Ambrose has commented that when Eisenhower pondered the decision to launch the invasion, he was the most powerful man on earth. Once he gave the "Let's go" order for June 6 a little after 4:00 on the previous morning, however, the General immediately became powerless to control events. The success or failure of Overlord was now up to the fliers, the paratroopers, the naval captains, the infantry officers, and the ordinary soldiers whose task it was to execute the plans. Eisenhower's two-word directive had unleashed the greatest land, sea, and air operation in history, but the result would be the work of countless thousands of "citizen soldiers."

The first fighters to hit the ground on D-Day were British paratroopers, sent in to secure the left flank of the attack front a few miles north of Caen. Their specific objectives were to neutralize the Merville battery, whose range commanded nearby Sword Beach, and to capture and hold bridges across the Orne River and its parallel Canal, near the villages of Ranville and Bénouville. Holding the bridges would not only deny the Germans use of them in moving troops against the British landing beaches, but it would make them available to the advancing British in their effort to seize Caen. These operations, undertaken by units from Britain's 6th Airborne Division, were amazingly successful. In the attack on the Orne Canal bridge, which today is known as Pegasus Bridge, three gliders managed to land with pinpoint accuracy, almost right on top of their objective. Major John Howard, who commanded the assault, remarked fifty years later that his company produced "arguably the best clockwork operation of D-Day."[21] Howard's forces were able to secure the bridge, and protect it from demolition, before the Germans knew what had hit them. The paratroopers, moreover, were able to hold the bridges against a determined German counterattack later in the day. Fighting had been nip and tuck at times, but the arrival of infantry units from Sword Beach relieved the airborne units and secured the area. The Café Gondrée, which still occupies the eastern side of the waterway at Pegasus Bridge, boasts of being the first house in France to be liberated on D-Day.

Similar success crowned the assault on the Merville battery and the nearby bridge across the Orne. The successes on the eastern flank were balanced, however, by the fact that Montgomery's troops had fallen short of taking Caen. That strategically vital transportation and communication center remained a fiery cauldron of battle well into July, when Anglo–Canadian forces finally drove the Germans out. This necessary step in the larger "breakout" would ultimately propel the Allied front to the Belgian frontier by the beginning of September. Frustrations over Montgomery's handling of the battle of Caen, nevertheless, ran particularly high in the American camp, and spirited debate about this subject continues in historical literature to this day.

On the other flank, sixty miles to the west, two American airborne divisions—the 82nd and the 101st—landed around midnight in the flat hedgerow country behind Utah Beach. Their objectives, much like those of their British counterparts, were to prevent the Germans from concentrating against the infantry landings and to facilitate the exit of Fourth Division troops from the beaches. Thick cloud cover, inexperienced pilots, and unexpectedly heavy flak conspired to disorganize this operation. Some paratroopers dropped too soon and drowned in the sea. Others dropped into areas that the Germans had flooded inland and drowned in three feet of water. Some came down in the middle of the village of Sainte-Mère Église, right onto a startled population—including German soldiers all too ready to shoot or capture them. The most famous of these errant paratroopers, John Steele of South Carolina, got hung up on the steeple of the village church—which today is still covered by a parachute—and was wounded in the foot by a German who shot him from the square below. All in all, the airborne divisions were scattered, as Stephen Ambrose puts it, "to Hell and gone."[22] But, as if Admiral Ramsey's prayer was being answered, the chaotic dispersal of the paratroopers, though it did nothing to facilitate the orderly formation of fighting units or to calm the fears of the young soldiers, probably worked in the attackers' favor. Receiving reports that airborne units were all over the southern end of the Cotentin peninsula and beyond—indeed, at least one American glider landed as far away as Saint Lô, over twenty miles behind Omaha Beach—the Germans thought they were under assault from a much larger force. Out of the disorder on the ground, and thanks to much successful individual combat among the forbidding hedgerows of the Cotentin hinterlands, the airborne fighters accomplished their strategic objective. When the Fourth Division landed on Utah Beach along the southeastern shore of the peninsula, it met extremely light resistance—suffering fewer than two hundred casualties—and immediately launched itself inland.[23]

The Fourth Division landing was not without its own fortuitous flaws. Upon reaching the shore at H-Hour, General Theodore Roosevelt, Jr. discovered that he had hit the beach roughly a mile below where he and his division were supposed to be. Faced with deciding whether to reposition the division or to proceed from where they were, Roosevelt resolved to "start the war from here"—and the landings continued on the wrong beach. But by arriving off-target, the division probably spared itself higher losses, for the Germans were capable of resisting more intensely farther north. General Roosevelt's willingness to make the best of a situation that had not gone according to plan was but one of the most famous of a host of such instances along the American beachheads that day.[24]

The next American action took place at Pointe du Hoc, a position on one-hundred foot cliffs that the Germans had fortified with guns capable of firing on both Utah and Omaha beaches. The seizure of this position was assigned to the Second Battalion of U.S. Rangers, about 225 men under the command of Lieutenant Colonel James Rudder. After beaching at the base of the cliffs on either side of the point, the Rangers scaled the cliffs using rope ladders and grappling hooks while under intense German fire. The first Rangers were up the cliff in less than ten minutes, and the position was secured after a fierce fight, during which most of the battalion was killed or wounded. What the men of Rudder's unit discovered at the top of the cliffs has been the source of considerable controversy ever since: The German guns were not in their mounts. It should not be concluded from this, however, that the operation was unnecessary or unimportant. The Rangers discovered the guns—readily capable of being moved to their mounts—a kilometer or so inland, where they had been hidden from Allied air attacks.[25] The weapons were immediately disabled so that they could not figure in enemy efforts to stop the landings. Pointe du Hoc, which was left just as it was at the end of the fighting on June 6, stands as one of the most impressive memorials in the Normandy landing areas.

Just a few miles east lies the most famous stretch of beachhead—code-named Omaha, and remembered by the men who fought there as "Bloody Omaha." The beach is five miles long, crescent-shaped, fronted by bluffs that stand as high as two-hundred feet above the shore, and hallowed by the sacrifice of the 2,500 Americans who died in the taking of it. By far, Omaha Beach saw the worst of the fighting on D-Day. And it was here that Operation Overlord came closest to failure.[26]

The Allied planners expected to subdue German resistance behind Omaha Beach with an intensive aerial and naval bombardment before the First Infantry Division, reinforced by units of the Twenty-Ninth Division, actually landed. Indeed, the bombs and shells were delivered, but the planes released their loads too far inland and the ships stopped their shelling before doing much damage to the German defenses. The ships would be heard from again later in the morning, in an improvised burst of shelling that played a crucial part in freeing the Americans from the beach. But the early waves of infantry landed into a veritable wall of steel. The attack quickly bogged down, and stayed that way deep into the morning. First-wave casualty rates at some sectors of the beach reached 85 percent, as entire boatloads of men perished before they could even fire their weapons.

The German division defending Omaha Beach—the 352nd Infantry Division—was the best coastal unit in Normandy. The Allies had not expected it to be where it was, and French Resistance operatives, who knew the truth about its position, had not been able to get this information to their London contacts. The 352nd had an elaborate array of barbed wire, minefields, trenches, and concrete emplacements—not to mention the formidable natural terrain—behind which to fight. About all that the initial waves of American soldiers could hope to do, in fact, was to get across the beach alive and find shelter at the base of the sand dunes at its top edge. The immobility of the initial arrivals on the beach created a blockage that forestalled the landing of later reinforcements. Indeed, two hours into the battle, the German commander on the scene reasoned that he had defeated the landing and chose not to call for reinforcements.

By mid-morning, however, with the help of destroyers that had moved dangerously close to shore to increase the deadliness of their fire, the Americans rallied and began to move up the bluffs. Holes were blown in the wire and sea walls that had stymied the initial advance, paths were created across the mined marshes, the enemy was rooted out of its trenches, and the guns guarding the bluffs were silenced.[27] Although the penetration inland by the end of the day was well short of Overlord's objectives, the Americans had at least established a relatively secure mile-deep hold on the beachhead, and the way was paved for a more or less constant flow of reinforcements in the days ahead. "Altogether," wrote Samuel Eliot Morison, "the Germans had provided [at Omaha Beach] the best imitation of hell for an invading force that Americans had encountered anywhere."[28] For a time, General Bradley had contemplated rerouting follow-up waves onto the British beaches, doubting that the logjam on Omaha could be broken in a timely manner. But in the end, the courage and resolve of the American infantry had simply carried the day.

The little town of Port-en-Bessin marked the division between the American and Anglo–Canadian beachheads. East of that line, the landings generally went easier. With the exception of Juno Beach, where the resistance was severe into mid-morning, the British and Canadians got ashore without substantial loss and attained deeper penetrations than the Americans by the end of the first day's fighting. Several factors were responsible for this. First, the quality of German troops behind those beaches was plainly inferior to that of the 352nd Infantry Division at Omaha. Second, the terrain at the eastern end of the attack front was not nearly so forbidding. Although the ground does rise behind sections of Gold, Juno, and Sword beaches, the inclines are much less steep than at Omaha. Third, the preliminary British naval bombardments lasted longer than the American bombardments, and took a greater toll on German defenses. Finally, the British made better use of amphibious tanks and armor on the beaches, and carried with them bundles of logs to ease their movement over the sea walls that fronted their landings.[29] By the end of the day, the trio of British and Canadian beaches were joined into a continuous lodgement area, a feat not to be achieved over the length of all five beaches until June 12. Still, at *none* of the code-named beaches were the troops able to attain on June 6 all of the objectives envisioned by the planners of D-Day.

If the success fell short of the planners' hopes, the D-Day invasion did punch a permanent hole in the Atlantic Wall, and proved a springboard for greater Allied triumphs in the months to follow.[30] Those follow-up triumphs would be hard-won, and would forever emblazon names like Caen, Saint Lô, and Falaise in the collective memory of the World War II generation, alongside the names associated with D-Day itself. But the undeniable fact at the end of June 6, 1944, was that Germany had undergone its "longest day," and its enemy was still on the beach. The decisive battle for the preservation of the Third Reich had begun, and the Allies had won the all-important opening engagement. Recalling his feelings on the evening of that first day, a German tank commander with the Panzer division closest to the Overlord front wrote:

> [I]t was . . . clear to the last man that the invasion had succeeded, that it could now be only a matter of days or weeks before the Allies would have landed sufficient forces to be able to mount an attack on Paris, and finally on the German Reich.[31]

Several days later, from Moscow, Stalin seemed to capture as well as anyone the significance of what the Allies had done:

> As is evident, the landing, conceived on a grandiose scale, has succeeded completely. My colleagues and I cannot but admit that the history of warfare knows no other like undertaking from the point of view of its scale, its vast conception, and its masterly execution. As is well known, Napoleon in his time failed ignominiously in his plan to force the Channel. The hysterical Hitler, who boasted for two years that he would effect a forcing of the Channel, was unable to make up his mind even to hint at attempt-

ing to carry out his threat. Only our Allies have succeeded in realising with honour the grandiose plan of the forcing of the Channel. History will record this deed as an achievement of the highest order.[32]

Fifty-seven years later, speaking on the occasion of the dedication of a national D-Day memorial in Bedford, Virginia,[33] the President of the United States, George W. Bush, called to mind the "scared and brave kids" who forced their way into Hitler's "Fortress Europe," and noted:

> The achievement of Operation Overlord is nearly impossible to overstate, in its consequences for our own lives and the life of the world. Free societies in Europe can be traced to the first footprints on the first beach on June 6, 1944.[34]

In a final tribute to the courage and the determination of these soldiers, President Bush observed: "Whatever it is about America that has given us such citizens, it is the greatest quality we have, and may it never leave us."[35]

Crowning the heights above Omaha Beach today, near the village of Saint Laurent-sur-Mer, is the Normandy–American Cemetery, the final resting place for over 9,300 of the American war dead from the Battle of Normandy. The ground of the cemetery has been ceded permanently by the people of France to the people of the United States for this purpose, and the dedicated staff of the American Battle Monuments Commission immaculately maintains the site. No one can visit there without being moved by its profound beauty, and by the silent statement it makes about the ultimate toll of battle. Indeed, I often say to my students that I have seen more grown men weep in Normandy than anywhere else. The major monument on the grounds, surrounded by a semicircular colonnade, is a bronze statue, "Spirit of American Youth," which depicts a young soldier rising from the waves to help liberate an oppressed continent. As undeniably glorious as that representation is, the row upon row of marble crosses and Stars of David facing it remind us of an equally inescapable fact: War cuts short the lives of young men.

Of the many tens of thousands who rose from the waves or descended from the skies on June 6, 1944, approximately ten thousand became casualties. Veterans thus remember the day with a mix of pride and deep sadness. Their summary recollections range from "the greatest thing I ever did in my life" to "the longest, most miserable, horrible day that I or anyone else ever went through."[36] When I once asked an H-Hour Omaha Beach veteran if he had ever been back to Normandy, he responded in a quiet voice: "No, I could never go back there. I left too many buddies back there." Many of his comrades probably feel the same way. But the most recent decennial commemorations, in 1984 and 1994, have seen large numbers of veterans return to re-live the "day of days" with their fellow soldiers and loved ones—to marvel at the feat, no doubt, and to mourn the cost. D-Day, then, will forever be remembered in different ways by the men who lived through it, as should be expected of any moment so laden with both triumph and tragedy.[37]

Perhaps the man who commanded Operation Overlord deserves the last word on this momentous event. This is so, not just because he successfully managed the immense undertaking, but because he understood so clearly why it was necessary and why so many were willing to follow him bravely into it. On June 6, 1964, as he gazed over Omaha Beach in the company of his interviewer, Walter Cronkite, General Eisenhower observed:

> [I]t's a wonderful thing to remember what those fellows twenty years ago were fighting and sacrificing for, what they did to preserve our way of life. Not to conquer any territory, not for any ambitions of our own. But to make sure that Hitler could not destroy freedom in the world. . . . It just shows what free men will do.[38]

Notes

1. John Keegan, *The Second World War* (New York: Viking Penguin, 1990), p. 5.
2. Forrest Pogue, "D-Day 1944," in Theodore A. Wilson, ed., *D-Day 1944* (Lawrence: University of Kansas Press, 1994), p. 180.
3. Carlo D'Este, *Decision in Normandy* (New York: E. P. Dutton, 1983), p. 13.
4. Omar N. Bradley, *A Soldier's Story* (New York: The Modern Library, [1951] 1999), p. 212.
5. Quoted in Max Hastings, *Overlord: D-Day, June 6, 1944* (New York: Simon & Schuster, 1984), p. 22. Churchill made this remark in a letter to President Franklin Roosevelt dated October 23, 1943.
6. Stephen E. Ambrose, *D-Day, June 6, 1944: The Climactic Battle of World War II* (New York: Simon & Schuster, 1994).
7. Quoted, ibid., p. 29.
8. Field Marshall Erwin Rommel to his aide, April 22, 1944, quoted in Cornelius Ryan, *The Longest Day* (New York: Popular Library, 1959), p. 8.
9. Quoted in Williamson Murray and Allan R. Millett, *A War to be Won: Fighting the Second World War* (Cambridge, MA: The Belknap Press of the Harvard University Press, 2000), p. 411.
10. Quoted in Gerhard L. Weinberg, *A World at Arms: A Global History of World War II* (New York: Cambridge University Press, 1994), p. 682.
11. In choosing Eisenhower for this post, President Roosevelt passed over the more senior Chief of Staff of the American Army, General George C. Marshall, to the latter's disappointment. But, the President believed, he could not spare General Marshall's extraordinarily able service in Washington. And, in Eisenhower, the Allies seem to have gotten a most successful mix of statesman and soldier to hold their coalition together and crush the German army. On Eisenhower as Supreme Commander, see Stephen E. Ambrose, *The Supreme Commander: The War Years of General Dwight D. Eisenhower* (Garden City, NY: Doubleday, 1970). The best work on General Montgomery, Eisenhower's often troublesome collaborator, is Nigel Hamilton's three-volume biography, with the volume pertinent to our discussion titled *Master of the Battlefield: Monty's War Years, 1942–44* (New York: McGraw-Hill Book Company, 1983).
12. Weinberg, *A World at Arms*, p. 681. See also Dwight D. Eisenhower, *Crusade in Europe* (New York: Doubleday, 1948), pp. 220–52, for a comprehensive discussion of the planning of Operation Overlord.
13. Two artificial "mulberry" harbors were to be located at Omaha Beach and Gold Beach (at the village of Arromanches). They were largely assembled and operating by the time a terrible Channel storm, which Eisenhower called a "hurricane," struck on June 19th. "Mulberry" A at Omaha Beach was irreparably damaged, while "Mulberry" B at Arromanches was repaired and kept in service. An excellent museum of this monumental engineering feat of the war resides in Arromanches today, and enough remnants of the harbor can still be seen to give one a very clear impression of the shape and scope of this undertaking.
14. Weinberg, *A World at Arms*, pp. 678–80.

15. Ibid., p. 684.

16. Eisenhower's Order of the Day for June 6, 1944, is excerpted in Ambrose, *D-Day*, p. 171. The full text is printed on the back cover of *D-Day to the Rhine Tour*, designed by Stephen Ambrose, a pamphlet available for purchase at the National D-Day Museum.

17. Ibid.

18. Admiral Ramsey's diary, June 5, 1944, quoted in ibid., p. 195.

19. Admiral Morton L. Deyo, quoted in Gerald Astor, *June 6, 1944: The Voices of D-Day* (New York: St. Martin's Press, 1994), p. 4.

20. Quoted in Ambrose, *D-Day*, p. 190.

21. John Howard, quoted in *Time* (International Edition), (June 6, 1994): 33. The best treatment of the battle for the Orne Canal bridge is Stephen E. Ambrose, *Pegasus Bridge* (New York: Simon & Schuster, 1985).

22. Stephen E. Ambrose, *Band of Brothers: E Company, 506th Regiment, 101st Airborne from Normandy to Hitler's Eagle's Nest* (New York: Simon & Schuster, 1992), pp. 70–88. See also Ryan, *The Longest Day*, pp. 128–44.

23. Ambrose, *D-Day*, pp. 275–319.

24. Ibid., pp. 275–93.

25. Ibid., pp. 398–417.

26. The most recent analysis of the fight at Omaha Beach is Adrian Lewis, *Omaha Beach: A Flawed Victory* (Chapel Hill: The University of North Carolina Press, 2001).

27. See Ambrose, *D-Day*, pp. 418–71. The Army's own account of the fight at Omaha Beach, published by the Historical Division of the War Department in 1945, is an invaluable aid in understanding this vitally important episode on D-Day. The booklet is titled *Omaha Beach (6 June–13 June 1944)* and is part of the "Armed Forces in Action Series."

28. The Morison quote appears in the introduction of Lewis, *Omaha Beach.*

29. Ambrose, *D-Day*, pp. 509–66.

30. In view of the fact that the German defenses along the D-Day beaches only held up the attacking Allies at most five or six hours, Ambrose concludes that the "Atlantic Wall must therefore be regarded as one of the greatest blunders in military history." Ibid., p. 577.

31. Hans von Luck, *Panzer Commander: The Memoirs of Colonel Hans von Luck* (New York: Dell Books, 1989), p. 180.

32. Quoted in Winston S. Churchill, *The Second World War*, abridged edition (London: Cassell, 1959), p. 784.

33. The 88-acre National D-Day Memorial was dedicated in Bedford, Virginia, on June 6, 2001. This small town in the mountains between Roanoke and Lynchburg suffered the highest per-capita death toll of any U.S. community on D-Day. Nineteen of Bedford's young men died in the first fifteen minutes of fighting for Omaha Beach and two more died later in the day. These twenty-one dead were from a total of thirty-five soldiers from Bedford who saw action on D-Day.

    The National D-Day Museum, founded by Stephen Ambrose and not to be confused with this memorial, is located in New Orleans and opened June 6,

2000. The Museum resides in New Orleans because this was the site of Andrew Higgins' factory that produced the landing craft ("Higgins Boats" or LCIs for "Landing Craft Infantry"), which ferried the assault troops from their transports to the beaches. General Eisenhower told Ambrose in 1964 that Higgins was "the man who won the war for us." (Ambrose, *D-Day*, p. 45.)

34. *Detroit Free Press* (June 7, 2001): Section A, pp. 4, 8.
35. Ibid., p. 8A
36. Astor, *Voices of D-Day*, p. 4; Ambrose, *D-Day*, p. 582.
37. Churchill titled the last volume of his six-volume history of the Second World War *Triumph and Tragedy* because, as he put it, "the overwhelming victory of the Grand Alliance has failed so far to bring general peace to our anxious world." (*Triumph and Tragedy*, p. vii.)
38. Quoted in Ambrose, *D-Day*, p. 583.

MILITARY UNPREPAREDNESS AND THE FAILURE TO KEEP THE PEACE: GREAT BRITAIN, 1919–1939

FREDERICK W. KAGAN

It is commonly believed in liberal democracies that preparation for war is something to be undertaken only when war is imminent or underway. Expenditure on the armed forces in peacetime, especially in periods of prolonged peace, is seen as wasteful and unnecessary. One reason for this is general ignorance of the vital role of peacetime military preparation as a deterrent. In the words of the old Roman saw: "If you want peace, prepare for war."

Few periods have borne out this fact more clearly than that between the two world wars of the twentieth century. The story of the failure of Great Britain's policy of appeasement in the 1930s is well-known; that of its military unpreparedness in the same decade somewhat less so. What has largely escaped the attention of historians and policymakers, however, was the critical role of Britain's military unpreparedness in the 1920s in creating the conditions for Britain's failed policies of the 1930s. Military unpreparedness is politically enervating. It leads to timidity and self-deterrence. It erodes the quality of the armed forces in a way not rapidly restored. And it can hinder

The opinions in this paper are those of the author and do not necessarily reflect the views or positions of any department or agency of the United States government.

or prevent essential military transformation. The story of Britain's failure to prevent World War II, and to succeed in its opening phases, must look beyond the policy of appeasement to the period in which another path could reasonably have been taken—but was not.

With the end of the First World War and the signing of the Treaty of Versailles, the leading democracies—Great Britain, France, and the United States—faced the burden of defending and maintaining the peace they had just made at great cost. Those states bore such a burden, because with the collapse of the Tsarist Empire in Russia, the Hohenzollern Empire in Germany, the Habsburg Empire in Austria, and even the Ottoman Empire in Turkey, they were the only remaining great powers. The peace itself, moreover, suited their worldview and interests, which was to be expected, since they had designed it and forced its acceptance on their vanquished foes.

The triumvirate of democratic victors soon broke apart, however, as the United States largely repudiated Woodrow Wilson's internationalism and withdrew into political and military isolationism. When the Senate refused to ratify the Treaty of Versailles or to permit America's accession to the League of Nations, it was clear that the United States would not be an active participant in the maintenance of the peace that its president had done so much to shape.

Between 1919 and 1923, it appeared that France and Britain might take up and shoulder this burden. Faced with a series of crises in the territories of the former Ottoman Empire, the Mediterranean, and scattered throughout Europe, these powers alternately accepted and eschewed the risk of small-scale conflicts as they tried to maintain the detailed terms of the peace without risking a major war. In the end, they failed in this effort, although they did avoid most small-scale conflicts. Thus an apparently bold British stand at Chanak, in 1922, produced a peace with Turkey that in no way resembled the Lloyd George government's initial terms. Britain's craven surrender to Mussolini's bluffs and machinations during the Corfu crisis went a long way in destroying the remaining respect English arms and power had the right to expect, following its sacrifices during the world war.[1]

Part of the reason for Britain's failure in those crises resulted from the fact that France was more eager to make deals with Turkey's Mustapha Kemal (Atatürk) and Italy's Mussolini than to support Britain's efforts to shape the postwar world in a positive way.[2] For their part, the French were far more concerned with enforcing the punitive terms of the Treaty of Versailles against Germany, convinced as they were that failure to enforce those terms would permit the ultimate restoration of superior German military capability and another German attack on France.

As it became increasingly clear that the Germans were working assiduously to undermine both the economic and the disarmament provisions of the Treaty, the French came to the conclusion that only direct action could save the peace. Accordingly, in 1923, they unilaterally invaded and seized Germany's Ruhr industrial region, working the mines with imported Frenchmen when the Germans ordered their workers to down tools. This gambit backfired. Although the Germans came to terms and entered new agreements regarding the payment of reparations, the unilateral invasion caused a serious rift between France and Britain, whose leaders were horrified at the thought of renewed hostilities over such apparently trivial issues.

The failure of Britain and France to see and accommodate each other's needs and interests thus played a powerful role in preventing either one separately, let alone both together, from actually supporting the peace. Britain's military unpreparedness to accomplish the tasks necessary to support the French or to maintain the peace on its own, however, was at least as important. France's defection during the Corfu crisis was serious, but not necessarily fatal, had Britain been able to face with equanimity the prospect of war with Mussolini. As it was, the Royal Navy's concern that war against Italy would leave British possessions in the Far East vulnerable to Japanese aggression was almost certainly exaggerated; but given a political leadership that had already demonstrated its unwillingness to pay for the expanded defenses needed to meet Britain's expanded commitments in the postwar world, the Navy's alarm was understandable.[3]

By 1923, the League of Nations had been thoroughly discredited, the Anglo–French entente was in danger of breaking up, America had withdrawn completely, and the Germans were aggressively and energetically preparing the basis for future rearmament—if not actually rearming—in direct contravention of the treaty they had signed. The prospects for long-term peace and stability were dim.

Still peace and stability remained in Europe until the early 1930s, and the costs of the failures of British and French policies in the 1920s were obscured for almost a decade. The relative wealth of the 1920s supported the devastated economies of Germany and the Soviet Union, keeping the former nominally democratic and the latter quiescent on the international stage. International opulence also supported the democratic Japanese government and helped it to mute the expansionist demands of a powerful militaristic bloc. Although the British preened themselves for bringing about such a state of affairs, their policies had little to do with it. In fact, they had set the stage for the catastrophe of the 1930s, by assuming that international stability and wealth would continue indefinitely without their involvement. When the peaceful international order unraveled dramatically between 1931 and 1933, the British were taken completely by surprise. What is even worse, they were entirely unprepared to respond.

The Legacy of the 1920s: Rearmament

Throughout the 1920s, Britain maintained its armed forces at a level that was inadequate to the requirements of its foreign policy. The basis of this neglect was not merely the well-known "ten year rule," but also the basic assumption underlying the re-establishment of the armed forces after demobilization. When considering the ultimate size to which the wartime armed forces should be reduced, the Lloyd George government assumed that the 1914 levels should be regarded as a ceiling. After all, it was argued, if there was any point in fighting the war, it was to make Britain safer; and if Britain was safer, then surely less costly defenses would be necessary. This assumption proved wrongheaded. For one thing, it ignored the fact that the British armed forces of 1914—especially the Army—had not been designed to fight Germany. The British Expeditionary Force that went to Belgium and was ground to virtually nothing in France had been built for imperial policing, not fighting on the continent. The collapse of Germany, then, was in principle irrelevant to the appropriate size of the British Army. Instead, in the years after 1918, the Army's size should have been based on an evaluation of the change in its mission.

Another problem with the Lloyd George government's assumptions was that the terms of the peace required the deployment of a considerable British force in the Rhineland for a significant period of time. British troops had not been maintained in continental Europe in peacetime in any significant numbers since the years following Waterloo, and nothing in its pre-1914 structure prepared the Army to handle such a mission. The collapse of the Ottoman Empire, moreover, left substantial tracts of Middle Eastern land in British hands as a League of Nations mandate. In most cases, these lands remained turbulent from the shock of the Ottoman collapse and the concomitant revival of internal tensions.

Another factor that greatly increased the requirements levied on Britain's armed forces was the lapse of the Anglo–Japanese alliance. Originally signed in 1902, this alliance had both the purpose and the effect of subcontracting the defense of Britain's interests in the Far East to a power seen as friendly and supportive of those interests. As a result, to the extent that Japan participated in World War I, it did so as Britain's ally; and although Tokyo did not generally pursue policies that London favored in that conflict, neither did it contemplate taking advantage of World War I to attack Britain's territories or interests directly. In the aftermath of the war, however, America became increasingly hostile to Japan and distrustful of the Anglo–Japanese alliance. In an effort to court American favor, therefore, Britain allowed the alliance to lapse. Suddenly, the Royal Navy had to take seriously the prospect of defending Britain's interests in the Far East without Japanese assistance, and even against Japanese opposition.[4]

In short, it should have been obvious that any comparison of force requirements in the 1920s to the force structure of 1914 was irrelevant, and that a thoroughgoing review of Britain's defense needs was urgently needed. The fact was that the 1914 force structure was both too small and too poorly organized to conduct the sorts of operations Britain faced in the early 1920s. One sees this in the series of manpower crises the Army faced after 1918 in trying to provide its component of the garrison of the Rhineland, suppress both the Iraqi rebellion and the Irish revolution, maintain peace in Palestine, and meet dozens of other smaller emergencies. At a number of points, the margin of safety approached zero—there were literally no reserves to be found anywhere in the British Empire. Nor was the British Army successful in its most significant missions: Ireland won its independence, the Iraq mission was transferred to the RAF, and the army on the Rhineland was known by the senior military leadership to be incapable of offensive action on even the smallest scale. This situation only deteriorated with the signing of the Locarno Treaty in 1925. Meant to placate French demands for an Anglo–French alliance without antagonizing Germany, this treaty committed Britain to fight on the side of France (or Germany) in the event of an unprovoked attack. The British Chiefs of Staff were quite clear throughout the discussions of the treaty that the British armed forces were incapable of meeting such an obligation. Still, nothing was done.

As the world settled down from the shocks of war and as the global economy continued strong, the consequences of Britain's military unpreparedness remained hidden. It was well-known to Britain's political leadership that Germany was violating numerous disarmament provisions of the Versailles Treaty, but the apparently peaceful trend of German foreign policy seemed to render such violations unimportant. In fact, throughout the latter half of the 1920s, basking in the glow of Locarno, it seemed that Britain would never face the reckoning for its inadequate military. But as the Great Depression struck Europe and Asia in 1930, the illusion of global stability evaporated. Within three years, the democratic façades of Germany and Japan were removed, as aggressive dictatorial regimes took power in Berlin and Tokyo. The Japanese armed forces announced both their political supremacy within Japan and their imperial designs with the invasion of Manchuria in 1931. Initially, the German threat was less clear, although no one much doubted that Hitler's accession to power in 1933 spelled danger.

It is beyond the scope of this essay to examine in detail the role of the economic downturn in the rise of dictatorial regimes in Germany and Japan, but its role was significant. The democratic governments in those states had been pursuing policies that were widely attacked by powerful constituencies for being subservient to the West and at variance with the "real needs" of the nation. They had maintained their power by promising—sometimes openly, sometimes secretly— to accomplish gradually, and perhaps peacefully, the aims of those aggressive constituencies, relying on the solid international economy for support. The economic collapse, therefore, discredited those democratic governments, even as it gave aggressive radicals new arguments in favor of their schemes.

The economic downturn also affected the United States and Britain. They did not turn away from their democratic traditions, of course. Instead, they turned away from the international scene. Horrified by the collapse of their standards of living, the U.S. and Britain turned to emergency measures to stop the bleeding and to restore their economic strength as rapidly as possible. The last thing they were worried about was what was going on elsewhere in the world, and the last issue they wanted to confront was the problem of how the economic slump affected the international military balance. As a result, the Japanese seizure of Manchuria—the most dramatic assault on the international order since the end of the First World War—was allowed to proceed by default. No major power ever seriously contemplated using force to oppose it in any way.

By 1933, the economic situation had bottomed out and was show-ing signs of recovery. At the same time, Hitler's rise to power in Ger-many set off clear alarm bells for some in London. The parlous state of Britain's defenses was finally recognized, and a committee was formed to study it and recommend solutions. When the Defence Requirements Committee sat down to work in 1933, however, its members were stunned by the magnitude of the task before them. They could not address the question of how to meet the new threats of Germany and Japan without first reckoning with the terrible shortfalls in the forces needed to conduct even the day-to-day business of securing Britain's interests in peacetime. Those shortfalls were severe and debilitating.

The Chiefs of Staff Subcommittee of the Committee of Imperial Defence had first raised the alarm about Britain's military unprepar-edness in its annual report for 1932. The military situation was ap-pallingly bad across the board. In the Far East—a region that acquired great importance when the Japanese seized Manchuria—the Chiefs reported,

> The position is about as bad as it could be. . . . In a word, we possess only light naval forces in the Far East; the fuel supplies required for the passage of the Main Fleet to the East and for its mobility after arrival are in jeopardy; and the bases at Singapore and Hong Kong, essential to the maintenance of a fleet of capital ships on arrival in the Far East, are not in a defensible condition. The whole of our territory in the Far East, as well as the coastline of India and the Dominions and our vast trade and shipping, lies open to attack.[5]

The Chiefs focused on the Far East in their report, they noted, be-cause "in those regions we are conceivably within measurable dis-tance of a catastrophe." But they went on to warn that, "As a matter of fact . . . we are equally unprepared for every major commitment that confronts the Services."[6]

The plan for the air defense of Great Britain, given relatively large emphasis during the 1920s because of the air attacks during World War I, was far from being executed. Although it had been decided that fifty-two squadrons were necessary to provide the offensive and defensive capabilities necessary to protect England, there were only forty-two squadrons in 1932—and thirteen of those were second-line. There was no anti-aircraft defense for the ports, and that of London itself was completely inadequate. The Chiefs recalled Balfour's comment of 1905: "We cannot sleep secure with only a bare margin of probability in our favour." But they added: "There is nothing approaching a bare margin today in the matter of defence against air attack."[7] Furthermore,

> For major military liabilities, such as might arise under the Covenant of the League of Nations or the Treaty of Locarno, we are but ill-prepared. In 1914 we intervened on the Continent with six well-equipped and well-trained Divisions within the first month of the War. If to-day we committed our Expeditionary Force to a Continental campaign in response to our liabilities under the Pact of Locarno, its contribution during the first month would be limited to one Division, arriving piecemeal; and except for the moral effect of its presence on the Continent, it could have little effect on the fortunes of the campaign. Even for a War for the defence of India or our other Eastern Possessions, this rate of mobilisation, which cannot be exceeded, would place us in a very difficult position.[8]

The objective of reducing the capabilities of the armed forces, if not their expense, below the level of 1914 had been achieved and exceeded.

The warnings in this 1932 annual report were not acted upon. Britain was still in the grip of the Depression, and the fiscal orthodoxy of the time ruled out the sort of government spending that was used with some success to "prime the pump" in the U.S. Therefore the Chiefs' report of 1933 was even more explicit about shortfalls in military preparedness:

> Our present resources do not permit us even to aim at anything better than to place in the field single divisions in each of the first two months of the war, a third at the end of the fourth month, and the remaining two divisions at the end of the sixth month. . . . [T]he demands for economy have prevented us from providing the modern equipment and the extremely important and expensive . . . reserves of ammunition which would be necessary for war on the continent of Europe, and even for a major contingency on the Frontiers of India. . . . The most we could do at present if called upon to intervene in Europe, and it is probably well-known to both our friends and enemies, would be to provide a small contingent of, say, one or at most two divisions at the outbreak of war, equipping them to a certain extent at the expense of later divisions preparing to go overseas.[9]

This report, coupled with Hitler's rise to power and a slight easing in the economic situation, had a significant impact. The Cabinet established the Defence Requirements Committee (DRC) to consider Britain's military deficiencies regarding the possibility of war in Europe, war in Asia, and war against the Soviet Union in India. It was explicitly instructed not to consider the possibility of war with Italy in the Mediterranean, since Italy was an ally in 1933.

The work of the DRC generated a great deal of worrisome detail. Even more worrisome was the daunting budget prediction that emerged as the price of the military unpreparedness of the 1920s. Sir Henry Pownall, one of the committee's secretaries, privately estimated that £145 million would be required, above and beyond already programmed defense budgets, to produce an adequate expeditionary force and territorial reserve.[10] The DRC could not bring itself to recommend such a figure, however, and called for the addition of only £71 million over five years for all of the services. The Army was to receive only £40 million of that increase.[11] Considering that the service budgets for 1933 had totaled only £108 million, the DRC's recommendation was daunting enough. Pownall's notion was politically unthinkable.[12]

The report immediately ran into an even more serious obstacle: British leaders had, by and large, learned only incomplete lessons from the First World War. Apart from the horror that trench warfare, and battles like Passchendaele and the Somme, had induced at the very idea of fighting on the continent, the war had convinced most intelligent people in most of the major powers that success in modern conflict depended at least as much on overall economic well-being as on fielded military forces. Thus, as the issue of rearmament came to the fore in the early 1930s, many British cabinet leaders, including especially Neville Chamberlain, believed that restoring and maintaining Britain's economic health was more important than rebuilding its armed forces. Some even hoped that the restored power of Britain's economy would, by itself, be great enough to deter hostile states. Since the financial convictions of the time argued that expenditures for nonproductive military purposes were economically harmful, this belief in the overriding importance of Britain's economic health militated powerfully against rapidly increasing defense budgets.[13]

There was a great deal of truth to the idea that economic strength was a critical element of national military power—a truth that was underlined once again during the ordeal that began for Britain on September 1, 1939. But the proponents of this argument ignored the important role that Britain could play in deterring aggressive states, and thereby in avoiding war or, at least, prolonging the peace. They ignored the fact that starving the armed forces in peacetime, in order to maintain economic strength for war, virtually ensured that war would come. Part of the appeal of this argument lay in the willful self-delusion of those politicians who were desperate to avoid thinking about, or preparing for, what they saw as an inevitable repetition of the mass slaughters of 1916–1918. For our purposes, however, it is

essential to recognize that the very magnitude of the resources needed to put right the deficiencies in Britain's armed forces played at
least as important a role.

The Cabinet showed, in 1934 and in subsequent years, that it
was willing to open the purse strings dramatically—at least relative
to normal peacetime military expenditure in a democracy. If the armed
forces had been sustained at a responsible level throughout the 1920s,
these increases in the 1930s might well have been enough to avert
war. As it was, the armed forces had been allowed to run down so far
in the 1920s that the DRC itself could not recommend the actual figure necessary to restore them, and the Cabinet modified even the
figure that was recommended. The Army received only £20 million
in place of the £40 million recommended—and of that, some £6.5
million was earmarked for anti-aircraft defenses.[14]

Parliament would vote vastly greater sums than those recommended by the DRC in 1934, but Britain never managed to rearm
adequately. The Minister for the Coordination of Defence, Sir Thomas
Inskip, reported in October 1938:

> By 1 August 1939 the re-equipment of the Regular Army
> should be virtually complete except for armoured fight-
> ing vehicles, anti-aircraft guns, and chemical warfare com-
> panies. But its scale of equipment and reserves would still
> be calculated on the basis of an Eastern theatre, a basis
> inadequate for the Continent. The present scale of equip-
> ment for the Territorial divisions would not even allow
> them to train effectively on embodiment. No fully equipped
> Territorial formation could take the field until at least eight
> months after the war began.[15]

The deficiencies Inskip noted had not been made good when the expeditionary force, against all expectation, actually did sail to the continent in September 1939. In July of that year,

[T]here were available only 72 out of 240 heavy anti-air-craft guns and only 30 percent of the approved scale of ammunition; only 108 out of 226 light anti-aircraft guns and 144 out of 240 anti-tank guns. . . . In August [1939] a War Office spokesman admitted that only 60 infantry tanks were available, against a total requirement of 1,646. As for training, there had been no large-scale Army manoeuvres for several years and Ironside [the commander of the BEF] had been counting on the September exercises to get I Corps into good order. As he gloomily noted in his diary, the units he had observed lacked even rudimentary tacti-cal skills. Thus in September the first four divisions of the Field Force sailed to France inadequately trained and short of every type of equipment, especially guns and tanks. The remainder of the growing citizen army at home was re-duced to "a token force of semi-trained troops" lacking the equipment for realistic training.[16]

The other armed services were in similar states of disarray. Although the RAF was expanding rapidly and had, almost acciden-tally, begun to develop and field both the radar and the effective fight-ers that would be needed to save England in 1940, it was still smaller than the Luftwaffe and inadequate to its various missions. The Navy was not capable of defending British interests in the Atlantic, the Far East, and the Mediterranean, even though it had been clear since 1935 that Italy was not friendly and, since the Japanese invasion of China in 1937, that conflict with Japan on the Asian periphery was likely. With that, Britain was extremely lucky. If the British Expeditionary Forces and other British services had been called upon to fight in September 1939, the result would likely have been a tragicomedy. As it was, almost nine months of "phoney war" passed before Hitler turned West, and more than two years of it before Japan attacked in the Far East. That Britain was able to put that time to good use does not alter the fact that had its enemies turned on Britain more rapidly than they did, the results would have been even more calamitous than they were.

The Legacy of the 1920s: Deterrence

The relationship between military capability and foreign policy is much closer than most democratic citizens recognize. Because they see diplomacy as a way of achieving the objectives of the state without using force, it is easy for them to ignore the critical importance of the capability to use force for the successful conduct of diplomacy. As George Kennan observed in 1946, "You have no idea how much it contributes to the general politeness and pleasantness of diplomacy when you have a little quiet armed force in the background."[17] When the aim of diplomacy is deterrence, the importance of having such an armed force—perhaps quiet, but certainly not too little—is greater by an order of magnitude. For Britain in the 1930s, the lack of such a force was a devastating diplomatic liability. At the same time, as the crises of the 1930s emerged and the possibility of the use of force was considered, it always seemed that using force would be very hard and dangerous, and that reliance on diplomacy and then appeasement would be easier and safer.

The Ethiopian Crisis of 1935 and Hitler's remilitarization of the Rhineland in 1936 are classic examples. In both cases, there is little question that Britain had the armed forces necessary to respond militarily. Italy's navy was in no way strong enough to stand off the Royal Navy, and Hitler himself was acutely aware of the magnitude of his gamble—later noting that if the British and the French had sent troops into the Rhineland to oppose him, he would have been forced to slink away with his tail between his legs. The problem was that in each case, the armed services made it clear to a fearful Cabinet that military action would be both difficult and dangerous, comforting the Cabinet in its timidity.

The British Chiefs of Staff have for too long managed to shirk their true responsibility for the disasters of the late 1930s by focusing attention on the failures of rearmament and the policy of appeasement. The Chiefs themselves were also to blame for consistently presenting the Cabinet with pessimistic estimates of what the armed forces could actually do. It is impossible to know, of course, what the Cabinet would have done in 1935 or 1936 if the Chiefs had reported the feasibility of fighting Italy or Germany. It is absolutely certain, however, that the reported infeasibility was a powerful factor in Britain's self-deterrence.

Why were the Chiefs so timid? For one thing, they were overwhelmed by the mismatch between Britain's global responsibilities and its military capabilities. During the Ethiopian crisis, the problem was not the Admiralty's doubt that the Royal Navy could defeat Italy, but its fear that Japan would take advantage of any setback or redeployment to attack Britain's Far Eastern possessions and interests. In more modern terms, we might say that Britain's lack of a two-major regional conflict capability led to self-deterrence in 1935.

Another part of the problem was that the Chiefs were so acutely aware of the deficiencies of the armed forces that they probably exaggerated, in their own minds, the difficulties of conducting any significant military operation. It is very difficult for a senior officer to recommend the use of force when he is not confident in the quality and readiness of the units being ordered into danger. It is not simply the fear that a botched operation will redound to the political disadvantage of his service (and himself), but also something more fundamental and honorable. Very few senior officers regard with complete equanimity the prospect of casualties among their troops. When lack of confidence in the troops' abilities leads such officers to the conclusion that casualties will be high, they are likely to resist the deployment. In this way, military unpreparedness creates an insidious force that predisposes senior officers against military operations. When military unpreparedness is coupled with strategic inadequacy, the result is usually a military dead-set against all military operations.

Considering that the Chiefs of Staff thought through all of the inadequacies of their services in 1934, in the context of the Defence Requirements Committee, it is not surprising that the predominant feeling among the leaders of the armed forces in 1935 was gloom. This observation is not enough to excuse their conduct. A truer understanding of their responsibilities and of the strategic situation should have led them to contemplate taking the risks necessary in the short-term on the chance of avoiding long-term crisis. Their failure is nonetheless understandable and their blame must be shared with their predecessors in the 1920s, both civilian and military, who allowed Britain's armed forces to come to such a pass.

This focus on the crises of 1935 and 1936 is not accidental. Those events were in many respects the pivotal moments of the crisis that led to war. In Ethiopia and the Rhineland, Italy and Germany could have been stopped relatively easily, and at least diverted from the path to Armageddon that Hitler appeared determined to pursue. Having failed in those initial tests, Britain (and France) actively encouraged further aggression. Worse still, as time went on, not only did the acts of aggression become more serious and dangerous, but the prospect of resisting them became ever more frightful, for Britain was engaged in a rearmament race with Germany which it was very likely to lose.

In the immediate aftermath of the Cold War, some argued that America could safely disarm because it could always rearm, if necessary, faster than its opponents. The British experience in the 1930s gives the lie to this happy thought. By 1933, Germany was no longer a democracy. There was no significant parliamentary check on Hitler's programs and, given his enormous popularity with the German people and the efficiency of his secret police, there was little popular check on his actions. As a result, Hitler was able to direct the resources of the German economy to rearmament at a level that was economically unsustainable and that probably would have led, sooner or later, to economic collapse. Even though the outbreak of the war came when the German armed forces were far from fully prepared, it did not come before they had made an amazing transformation, both in quantity and in quality: In 1933, Germany had no modern ground forces; in 1940, seven German armored divisions destroyed the Anglo–French armies.

The British could not hope to match this pace of rearmament. Nor did they, as the following table shows:

Percentage of GNP Devoted to Military Expenditure in Great Britain and Germany, 1932–1940[18]

Year	Great Britain	Germany
1932	3	1
1933	3	3
1934	3	6
1935	3	8
1936	4	13
1937	6	13
1938	7	17
1939	18	23
1940	46	38

Since GNP figures can sometimes be misleading as to total amounts, we should note that, in sum, Germany spent approximately three times as much as Great Britain on rearmament between 1933 and 1938.[19] There were, of course, a wide variety of factors that led to this disparity. But the simple fact that a dictatorial regime can, more easily than a democracy, devote a far greater proportion of its resources to any single task was one of the most salient. The notion that democracies are able to rearm faster is historically unsupported.

As the crisis between England and Germany reached its climax at the end of the 1930s, therefore, Britain's military situation had only deteriorated. When Hitler threatened Czechoslovakia in 1938, he could have been resisted. In fact, a coalition of Czechoslovakia (not at all a negligible military power), France, and Britain would not have had the slightest difficulty in stopping Hitler cold. But Britain's political leaders had become mesmerized by the rising power of the Luftwaffe—whose strength they grossly overestimated in their fear— and its military leaders were horrified by the prospect of sending their ill-trained and ill-equipped legions into combat. Nor were they entirely wrong to be fearful, for when Britain's forces deployed to the continent in September 1939, they were completely unready to wage war.

Military Unpreparedness and the Collapse of the Peace

Military unpreparedness was not the root cause of Britain's failure to keep the peace in the 1930s. The root cause of that failure was the unwillingness of Britain's leaders to recognize their responsibilities. They had convinced themselves in the aftermath of the First World War that the peace would keep itself, helped along by international organizations like the League of Nations and by their own half-hearted diplomatic commitments, such as the Treaty of Locarno. They imagined that the resort to military force, which horrified them, would remain unnecessary into the indefinite future. Britain's military unpreparedness was epiphenomenal to that mindset. Still, it gravely complicated Britain's efforts to respond to the collapsing situation in the mid-1930s. The fact that the armed forces were so inadequate even to their peacetime tasks meant that "rearmament" in Britain first required the restoration of what should have been present in peace. Only then could Britain's leaders think about arming to meet the rising German threat—and by then it was far too late.

Democracies, on the whole, prefer disarmament in peacetime. Only in the presence of imminent threats, real or perceived, do their leaders usually call for—and the electorate usually support—increases in defense spending. But, armed forces that have once been dismantled can usually be restored only slowly and painfully. As a consequence, the record of democracies deterring large-scale aggression is abysmal. Britain before World War I and World War II, America before Pearl Harbor and before the North Korean attack in 1950, and many other examples serve to demonstrate this point. In each case, the would-be aggressor perceived the democracy's temporary weakness and lack of will. In most of these cases, the aggressor also saw that the slow rearmament of the democracy would, over time, make a successful attack unlikely. Far from deterring attack, therefore, the democratic pattern of rearmament actively encourages aggression. Thus when war actually comes, democracies are usually unprepared. Precisely because aggressors see their window of opportunity closing, they attack while it is still open—that is, while the democratic states are still unprepared. It is no accident that Hitler opted for war in 1939; he believed that by 1941, Britain would be too strong.

There is a way to avoid this trap, of course, and that is to maintain adequate armed forces in peacetime. Such a course of action eliminates the window of opportunity and provides a credible force to back up the policy of deterrence that is favored by democracies. In the worst case, where deterrence has failed and war has come, military preparedness increases the chance of victory. It is unfortunate that the Western democracies have repeatedly failed to learn these lessons, and, indeed, that these lessons have been so often repeated. The present situation offers little indication that the dismal pattern of democratic behavior during the twentieth century has been altered.

Notes

1. See Donald Kagan and Frederick W. Kagan, *While America Sleeps: Self-Delusion, Military Weakness, and the Threat to Peace Today* (New York: St. Martin's Press, 2000), chapters 3 and 4 for detailed discussions of the Chanak Crisis and chapter 5 for the Corfu crisis.
2. It must be admitted that the initial British objectives during the crisis with Turkey were not necessarily either reasonable or attainable, and that the settlement that emerged from the crisis proved to be a great deal more

durable and positive for the region than anything that was likely to have emerged had Lloyd George had his way. French policies, nevertheless, did not reflect any straightforward substitution of intelligent policies for ill-advised ones, but rather an effort to come to terms with Atatürk in order to further France's position in the Middle East even at the expense of Britain.

3. See Kagan and Kagan, *While America Sleeps*, chapters 1 and 2 for a discussion of the crisis in defense policy in the years immediately following World War I. This crisis had not affected the Navy as drastically as it had the other two services, but then again the Navy had not really had to face up to the possible dangers until the Corfu Crisis, whereas the Army's limitations had been apparent in 1919. The RAF's problems, paradoxically enough, only became clear during the crisis that followed the French occupation of the Ruhr, when the putative air power enemy was taken to be France!

4. This is not to say that the Admiralty was very quick to evaluate the consequences of this change in affairs. In fact, right up until the Japanese invasion of Manchuria most British policymakers seemed convinced that the effects of the Anglo–Japanese alliance would persist indefinitely even in the absence of the alliance itself. The Japanese, for their part, insulted by London's rebuff, took another view.

5. Committee of Imperial Defence, Chiefs of Staff Sub-Committee, "Imperial Defence Policy: Annual Review for 1932 by the Chiefs of Staff Sub-Committee," C.O.S. 295, CAB 53/22, pp. 273ff, p. 4.

6. Ibid.

7. Ibid.

8. Ibid.

9. Committee, "Imperial Defence Policy: Annual Review (1933)," CAB 52/23, pp. 11–12.

10. Brian Bond, *British Military Policy Between the Two World Wars* (New York: Oxford University Press, 1980), p. 199.

11. N. H. Gibbs, *History of the Second World War, United Kingdom Military Series: Grand Strategy: vol. 1, Rearmament Policy* (London: Her Majesty's Stationery Office, 1976), p. 98.

12. Ibid., p. 532.

13. See G. C. Peden, *British Rearmament and the Treasury: 1932–1939* (Edinburgh: Scottish Academic Press, 1979), passim, but especially Chapter III, "The Treasury's Influence on the Financial Limits to Rearmament."

14. Bond, p. 207.

15. Ibid., p. 288.

16. Ibid., pp. 328–29.

17. Cited in John Lewis Gaddis, *Strategies of Containment* (New York: Oxford University Press, 1982), p. 39.

18. Peden, p. 8.

19. Ibid.

GENERAL GEORGE S. PATTON
AND THE SPIRIT OF WESTERN WARFARE

VICTOR DAVIS HANSON

"A swaggering big mouth, a Fascist aristocrat." So John Philips summed up George S. Patton in the *New York Times*. Andy Rooney has been on occasion even more vehement: "I detested Patton and everything about the way he was." Dwight MacDonald concluded that Patton was "brutal and hysterical, coarse and affected, violent and empty."[1]

That gallery of civilian invective—mostly in response to Patton's public bombast and famed bellicosity—was trumped by military analysts and fellow officers alike who faulted everything from his demeanor to his generalship. "I think he was about half mad," wrote the military historian S. L. A. Marshall. "Any man who thinks he is the reincarnation of Hannibal or some such isn't quite possessed of all his buttons." Charles Whiting was more analytical in his condemnation: "Nor was he a Great Captain. . . . He fought no decisive battle such as Montgomery did at El Alamein, or the unknown General Alexander Patch in Alsace. . . . Not once did he fight a set-piece battle successfully." Omar Bradley, who often posed as an intimate

---

Portions of four pages from Victor Davis Hanson, *Soul of Battle* (New York: Free Press, 1999) have been incorporated into this essay.

and supporter, concluded that Patton's untimely demise on December 21, 1945, was, in fact, opportune: "He would have gone into retirement hungering for the old limelight, beyond doubt indiscreetly sounding off on any subject any time, any place. In time he probably would have become a boring parody of himself—a decrepit, bitter, pitiful figure, unwittingly debasing the legend."[2]

Few American generals have invoked such a visceral response as George S. Patton. What precisely accounts for such controversy so many years after the general's death? His mercurial temperament and brutal candor are, of course, legendary—as is his profanity. A few months of near-lunatic pronouncements during his brief proconsulship of Bavaria from May to November 1945—strange ramblings about "the non-Aryan press," communists, conspiracies, and Nazis—only cemented earlier doubts about his stability. These doubts had been raised when he slapped two shell-shocked soldiers, and continued through an array of what are now recognized as relatively minor escapades, such as shooting two Sicilian mules and slandering Russian communists in public speeches. In this regard, Patton's ego and showmanship ostensibly put him in the category of a MacArthur, his crudity on level with a LeMay. A contemporary radio broadcast summed up the emergence in Normandy of the very public and profane Patton:

> As Patton has said, "You can't run an army without profanity." As his men say, "You've never lived until you have been cussed out by General Patton." Veterans of the African campaign used to say when they heard a demolition charge explode nearby: "That's General Patton telling General Eisenhower—in confidence." Back in the days when Patton first started to climb in Army rank his friends warned him to tone down his speech. As he said then: "I've got to be dignified, damnit."[3]

Yet while Patton's behavior and often strange and repugnant outbursts in nonmilitary matters account for much of the lasting variance in opinion about his legacy, they do not explain all of the controversy he aroused and the jealousy he incurred. In addition, it was Patton's unique approach to war—especially his ambiguous relationship with traditional Western notions of direct attack and frontal assault— that was so disturbing to a number of influential contemporaries.

What is the Western Way of War?

The Western way of warfare could be characterized by a variety of military protocols which allowed European armies, from the Greeks to those of the present day, to exercise dominating military power not commensurate with either their limited territories or populations. Much of Western military dynamism involves the use of superior technology, which is the product of free inquiry and a rationalist tradition. In comparison to other cultures, Western scientific research and development have been relatively unimpeded by either religious or political constraints. Capitalism, consensual government, civic militarism, strong notions of individualism coupled with group discipline, as well as civilian oversight of military operations and a general tolerance of freewheeling self-critique, have also ensured that Western armies were usually better supplied, armed, organized, and led than their opponents, and often more flexible in response and receptive to change. Yet another key characteristic of the Western military tradition has been to seek out the enemy in open confrontation, often through decisive infantry collisions with less trust in ruse or deception.[4] In the case of the propensity for shock battle, the free Greek city-states bequeathed to us the idea that states might wage war in daylight, head-on, and en masse, thereby deciding conflict decisively and without delay. In a famous and much quoted passage, the historian Herodotus made the Persian commander Mardonius caricature precisely this Hellenic preference for such showdowns:

> The Greeks, as I have learned, are accustomed to wage wars
> in the most stupid fashion due to their silliness and folly.

For once they have declared war against each other, they search out the finest and most level plain and there fight it out. The result is that even the victors come away with great losses; and of the defeated, I say only that they are utterly annihilated.[5]

Alexander the Great inherited this peculiar affinity for open engagement. Before the Battle of Gaugamela, the historian Curtius recorded that Alexander worried only that Darius might not fight. When awoken on the day of the battle, Alexander was purportedly relieved: "When Darius was torching the countryside, burning villages and destroying the food supply, I was beside myself. But now, what do I have to worry about since he is preparing to fight it out in open battle? By God, he has satisfied my every wish." Plutarch adds that Alexander also asked, "What is the matter? Don't you think that now we already appear to have won, since no longer do we have to wander about in a vast and denuded country in pursuit of a Darius who avoids pitched battle?"[6]

Roman legions usually followed suit, if on occasion demonstrating far greater flexibility and more tactical options than had the more unwieldy phalanx. Nor did the classical legacy of civic militias and shock battle end with the collapse of Rome; heavy infantrymen and citizen soldiers reemerged from time to time among the Franks, Swiss, and Italians, who fielded phalanxes of pikemen that proved invincible on medieval and Renaissance battlefields. Even the introduction of firearms did not change the classical reliance on group cohesion, close order, and decisive battle, as Westerners alone learned to fire on cue and in formation, and to define discipline as the maintenance of rank, fire control, mastery of drill, and protection of one's comrades nearby. In comparison, individual kills or acts of weapon prowess were rarely the basis for official commendation.[7]

Within this larger strategic and tactical landscape, Western generals were originally judged on their commitment to take their deadly infantry columns into decisive battle. Before the age of Alexander, anonymity characterized Greek leaders, who fought in the front ranks of the phalanx and led their men head-on against the enemy. In Roman times, few defeated commanders were ever castigated for stupidity, as long as they could demonstrate that they had at least forced the enemy into a decisive confrontation. The relatively benign reception at Rome of the imbecilic Varro, in the aftermath of the slaughter at Cannae, suggests that the consul-general escaped censure simply because he had not fled or delayed battle, and had at least illustrated Roman audacity and determination by leading his men directly into Hannibal's noose. In many of the Greek city-states, elected generals were not judged as tacticians or grand strategists as much as drillmasters, whose duty was to muster troops and lead them directly against enemy armies. As a rule, there is not a recorded instance in classical literature—at least pertaining to any of the major city-states during the fifth and fourth centuries B.C.—of a defeated Greek general abandoning his men, or even surviving the battle.[8]

It became a truism, then, that early Western battle leaders were rather anonymous wardens of a superior system of discipline and organization. And for centuries following, in intracultural wars against Persians, Carthaginians, Muslims, Ottomans, and tribes and civilizations of Africa and the Americas, European commanders often relied on their own troops' superior training, technology, and discipline to win decisive battles; the system, rather than tactical brilliance, was felt adequate to trump enemy numbers, surprise, and bad luck. For the most part, in wars against the "other," such a reliance on tried protocols, coupled with an eagerness to initiate horrific engagements, proved successful, from the battle of Plataea to the nineteenth-century colonial wars in Africa.

When Western armies turned upon each other, however, decisive battle—Waterloo, Verdun, the Battle of the Bulge—was a different story altogether. More often than not, mutual carnage was the result, rather than a one-sided shattering of enemy ranks. More Greeks died in single battles of the Peloponnesian War than all the infantry casualties incurred in the Persian Wars. For two centuries, Greek and

Macedonian losses against the Persians—at battles from Marathon to Gaugamela—were a fraction of those incurred at the terrible fighting at Mantinea, Nemea, Coronea, or Chaeronea. Caesar's army, which had butchered thousands in Gaul, found war far different when they fought Pompey and his sons. Waterloo was unlike anything Napoleon had experienced in Egypt. The British would discover, mere decades after their colonial victories, that the Germans in France were not the same caliber of enemy as had been the Sudanese or Zulus. Still, despite the brutality of modern intra-Western warfare, Napoleon, Lee, Grant, Pershing, Haig, Foch, Joffre, and others established their reputations by initiating decisive battles, seeking to kill as many soldiers as possible and to break the will of the enemy army through a series of concentrated hammer-blows. Patton's rather different emphasis on outmaneuvering his rivals caused General Leslie McNair to scoff, during army exercises in 1941, "This is no way to fight a war." This was echoed by Reuben Jenkins in his *Military Review* broadcasts: "The price of victory is hard fighting and . . . no matter what maneuver is employed, ultimately the fighting is frontal." Russell Weigley, in summing up the American propensity for decisive battle, noted, "At the beginning, when American military resources were still slight, America made a promising beginning in the nurture of strategists of attrition; but the wealth of the country, and its adoption of unlimited aims in war, cut that development short, until the strategy of annihilation became characteristically the American way in war."[9]

The Heterodoxy of the Indirect Approach

Within this general Western emphasis on power, and on the discipline and courage of a system rather than the genius of a Great Captain, there has always been a counter tradition of more sophisticated tactical and strategic thought. This latter sought to direct military operations away from simple frontal attacks, both by outmaneuvering and outflanking enemy armies in the field and by directing larger

operations against the enemy homeland, in efforts to undermine civilian morale and to destroy sources of logistical support. Liddell Hart, a
veteran of the holocaust of World War I trenches, devoted an entire
book to what he called the "indirect approach." In the past, according
to Hart, the more common strategies of annihilation favored by European generals had brought stalemate and carnage, while the rarer use
of flexibility and movement led to strategic victory. "Throughout history," he wrote,

> the direct approach has been normal, and a purposeful in-
> direct approach the exception. It is significant, too, how often
> generals have adopted the latter, not as their initial strate-
> gy, but as a last resource. Yet it has brought them a decision
> where the direct approach has brought them failure. . . .[10]

In this context, one thinks not just of the likes of Caesar, Alexander, and Scipio, who were blasters as well as maneuverers, or even
of brilliant commanders of trained commandos and irregulars from
Brasidas and Chabrias to Francis Marion and Nathan Bedford Forrest, but also of directors of great marches involving thousands of
men, such as Epaminondas, Sherman, and Rommel. The latter, at
various times, relied on speed, ruse, and attacks at an enemy's rear
or base of operations to change the complexion of entire theaters of
operation. Generals like Sherman or Patton realized that war between
two Western powers, fought in the tradition of frontal assaults with
highly disciplined, well-armed Western forces—whether at Shiloh,
the Somme, or the Hedgerows of Normandy—resulted in abject
slaughter for both sides, and thus demanded alternatives.

Despite the success of such mavericks, suspicion always lingered
that they were not real commanders who could face up to enemy blows
and destroy the opposition on the field of battle. Notwithstanding
the horrific nature of frontal assault, Westerners have felt more
comfortable with commanders like Grant, Lee, Haig, Pershing, Eisenhower, and Bradley, who reflected orthodoxy by seeking primarily to

find the enemy army and to destroy it through reliance on superior discipline, organization, and technology. In consequence, to combat such forces of tradition and entrenchment, as well as the lingering suspicion of the "indirect approach," iconoclasts often deliberately sought to adopt a compensating persona that stressed the violence and brutality of face-to-face killing. While their favored method of war was not aimed at slaughtering enemy soldiers per se, their rhetoric reflected it. In this regard, Patton's obnoxious rants—rather than revealing inner psychological turmoil, past brain injury, or innate character flaws—were just as likely intended to impress Eisenhower, Bradley, and the American public that his fast-moving, enveloping columns were eager and capable of engaging German divisions in the favored American tradition of battles of annihilation.

In a similar manner, Epaminondas, the fourth-century B.C. general of the Boeotian confederation, bragged that he would tear down the Athenian Propylaea should Athens oppose his plans. He was said to have killed sleeping guards with his own hands, shouted down the Spartan king at a peace conference, and warned his Theban citizens that constant preparation for war was the only guarantee of peace. Yet this firebrand's greatest achievement was not the stunning infantry victory against the Spartans at Leuctra in 371 B.C.—the Thebans, after all, had beaten or withstood the Spartans on at least three prior occasions—but his great march into Laconia, the freeing of the Helots, the creation of a liberated Messenia, and the founding of the great fortress at Messene. That great trek of 370–69 B.C., however, saw no real pitched battles and led to few casualties. Instead, through marches, terror, and attacks on Laconian infrastructure, Epaminondas had done in six months what Athens could not accomplish in twenty-seven years—despite thousands of casualties, near constant campaigning, and the eventual collapse of the entire Athenian empire itself. From what little we know of the life of Epaminondas, he seems to have been as bellicose, controversial, and mystical a character—contemporaries claimed he was a Pythagorean—as Patton.[11]

So too Sherman's outbursts are legendary, ranging from vows to kill hundreds of thousands of Southerners and to exterminate outright the aristocratic cavalry class of the Confederacy, to threats of hanging snooping reporters and burning entire cities. Yet his record during the last year of the Civil War tells a story of achieving victory "more by the movement of troops than by fighting." Between November 1864 and April 1865, Sherman marched over five hundred miles through Georgia and the Carolinas, destroyed hundreds of millions of dollars in Confederate property—mostly the plantations of the rich, railroads, communications, and public buildings—and overcame, in a humiliating way, feeble Confederate efforts at resistance. Nevertheless, controversy still rages about Sherman's exact military achievement: Those who dwell on his rhetoric and on the toll of his devastation of Southern property call him a monster, even as military historians often complain that he was an inexperienced battle tactician who rarely squared off in a traditional engagement.[12]

Irony abounds. A taciturn Grant butchered both Southern manhood and sent thousands of his own on ruinous frontal charges. Yet he never incurred the degree of odium of the property-destroying Sherman. A beloved and soft-spoken Lee wrecked his army in a Northern invasion, killed thousands, and prolonged the war. Indeed, in almost every instance, Lee's incursion into Pennsylvania was the opposite of the hated Sherman's march to the sea. Lee killed thousands and lost thousands in a vain effort to change the course of the war in the North, while Sherman brought the war to a close in the South at little cost to his or the enemy's soldiers. Such is the dominant influence of the Western way of warfare, that we castigate as murderous those who kill few and praise as heroic those who butcher many.

Patton: Rhetoric and Reality

Patton shared the same ambiguous relationship to traditional Western battle as had Epaminondas and Sherman. As a corps and army group commander in North Africa, Sicily, and Europe, Patton quickly surmised the costs involved in a collision with seasoned German troops, whose discipline, equipment, and command were equal if not superior to that of American troops. It was not that he doubted that American men and materiel could overwhelm the Nazis in shock battles, but that he knew such successful collisions would require an inordinate sacrifice of American blood. Instead, on the eve of his deployment in Normandy, Patton outlined the method of Third Army attacks to come, punctuating vulgarity with what in fact was a radical and enlightened alternative to the traditional preference for head-on assaults:

> There's another thing I want you to remember. Forget this goddamn business of worrying about our flanks. . . . Some goddamned fool once said that flanks must be secured and since then sons of bitches all over the world have been going crazy guarding their flanks. We don't want any of that in the Third Army. Flanks are something for the enemy to worry about, not us. I don't want to get any messages saying that, "We are holding our position." We're not holding anything! Let the Hun do that. We are advancing constantly and we're not interested in holding on to anything except the enemy. We're going to hold on to him by the nose and we're going to kick him in the ass; we're going the kick the hell out of him all the time and we're going to go through him like crap through a goose. . . . We have one motto, "L'audace, l'audace, toujours l'audace!" Remember that gentlemen.[13]

In compensation for his preference of the indirect approach ("hold on to him by the nose and kick him in the ass"), Patton took equal pains to stress the lethality of his army, as if its rapid marches still signified a willingness to kill Germans:

> I want them [the Germans] to look up and scowl, "Ach, IT'S THE GODDAMN THIRD ARMY AND THAT SON-

OF-A-BITCH PATTON AGAIN!" We want to get this thing over and get the hell out of here, and get at those purple-pissin' Japs!!! The shortest road home is through Berlin and Tokyo! We'll win this war, but we'll win it only by showing the enemy we have more guts than they have or will ever have. There's one great thing you men can say when it's all over and you're home once more. You can thank God that twenty years from now, when you're sitting around the fireside with your grandson on your knee and he asks you what you did in the war, you won't have to shift him to the other knee, cough, and say, "I shoveled shit in Louisiana."[14]

In the schizophrenic world of George Patton, calls to avoid the main body of enemy resistance were often rejoined by coarse appeals for face-to-face killing. At bayonet practice, he pointed to a dummy and screamed to his men, "That's a German. You don't hate him enough. You're all too gentlemanly. Just because you've been brought up not to kick your grandmother in the ass, don't think he hasn't, because he has—they all have.... For the present just keep hating Germans."[15] Yet to place Patton's achievement in its proper military and cultural context, we must dwell not on what he said, but on what he did, realizing that his rhetoric of death and killing was the necessary cargo of his tactical unorthodoxy and humanity in avoiding needless bloodshed.

During his ten months in Europe, between August 1944 and May 1945, there were at least four occasions when Patton's calls for speed, maneuver, and flexibility, if followed, may well have shortened the war. In each instance, Patton's own characterizations of his rapid maneuvers were usually presented in the crude language of killing and brutal assault, and were dismissed as either showmanship or vulgarity by his superiors—only later to be seen as brilliant operations by sober historians in the war's aftermath.

The first instance surrounds the controversy over the Allies' great encirclement of Hitler's Army Group B at the so-called Argentan–Falaise gap in early August of 1944. Patton, worried about the difficult progress of Canadian forces in their efforts to reach Falaise, ordered his XV Corps to go beyond the agreed-on boundary at Argentan, meeting the Canadians further to the northeast and thereby closing the last escape route for several German divisions. "We should go on," he exclaimed at reaching Argentan. "There's nothing out there. Nothing between me and the Seine." Patton, hoping to unleash his tanks into the British sector, then exclaimed, "Let me go to Falaise and we'll drive the British back into the sea for another Dunkirk." Yet Bradley balked. "Nothing doing," he ordered Patton. "Don't go beyond Argentan. Stop where you are and build up on that shoulder." Patton was dumbfounded. The next day, August 13, he tried again for permission to press north from Argentan, this time with Bradley's assistant Leven Allen: "Have you talked with Brad?" The answer was the same. "Yes, George. The answer is always no."[16]

Patton turned to his staff officers and ordered: "The question why XV Corps halted on the east–west line through Argentan is certain to become of historical importance. I want a stenographic record of this conversation included in the History of the Third Army." Later, Patton recorded at length Bradley's stop order at Argentan in his diary:

> It was perfectly feasible to continue the operation. Allen repeated the order [from Bradley] to halt on the line and consolidate. I believe that the order emanated from 21st Army Group, and was either due to jealousy of the Americans or to utter ignorance of the situation or to a combination of the two. It is very regrettable that the XV Corps was ordered to halt, because it could have gone on to Falaise and made contact with the Canadians northwest of that point and definitely and positively closed the gap.[17]

Apparently, Patton had been ordered to stop his XV Corps at Argentan because of Bradley's fear that American armor might either meet head-on friendly Canadian troops, slowly descending from the north, or be steamrolled by desperate Germans heading east. As a result, during the ensuing week before the noose was finally closed on August 19, an enormous force of 175,000 to 200,000 surrounded German troops had a fifteen-mile corridor of escape between encircling Allied armies. Bradley later sought to characterize Patton's plans for a complete envelopment as rash and ill-considered. In his memoirs, after quoting Patton's jest about Dunkirk, he first blamed Montgomery for the halt; then, extraordinarily, he bragged that he had stopped Patton from a "brash and foolish overextension!" He somehow claimed all at once that Patton's advance beyond Argentan would be "a slap in the face" to the Canadians marching from the north; that Patton had infuriated Bradley with his "boastful, supercilious attitude"; that he preferred "a solid shoulder at Argentan to the possibility of a broken neck at Falaise"; and that the Germans were already mostly escaping and ready for a counterattack.[18]

We now know, of course—as Bradley must have known when he wrote his memoirs—that Montgomery sought to close the gap, but that the Canadians were having difficulties and wished for succor; that Patton was reasonable, not boastful, in his desire to push on; that there was little chance of a broken neck; and that the Germans on August 13, 1944, were *not* mostly gone and *not* planning a counterattack, but disorganized, trapped, and desperate. Hubert Essame put the tragic decision at Argentan in the context of the Allied effort to end the war in 1944:

> Posterity, with its knowledge of the actual plight of the Germans at the time denied to Eisenhower, may justifiably conclude that the complete annihilation of the Germans could have been achieved and a decision reached which might well have enabled the war to be ended in 1944. Patton and Haislip, with the 2nd French Armoured Division, 5th Armored Division and the rest of XV Corp...had it within their power to fight a decisive action at half-price in

terms of American life. Argentan might have been as great
a battle honor in the annals of the American Army as Second Manassas or Chancellorsville.[19]

Of some 80,000 to 110,000 German soldiers trapped in the actual pocket, at least 50,000 escaped. While there were probably almost
nineteen German divisions ruined in or near Falaise, a good chance
was lost to eliminate, in one fell swoop, at least 100,000 Germans—
and perhaps another 150,000 to the north and south. But the missed
opportunity was not merely quantitative in terms of soldiers and
equipment; if an entire German army could have been annihilated,
the shock of that catastrophe would have rippled throughout the
Western front, leaving the Allies free to race through a relatively undefended France into a poorly defended and stunned Germany.[20]

Patton alone seemed to grasp the lost opportunity. Thus he
immediately raced farther east to the Seine River in an attempt to sal-
vage the envelopment, seeking a second chance at an even wider en-
trapment of the fleeing German Seventh Army and Fifth Panzer Army.
By August 16, Third Army corps were in Chartres and Orléans, on
their way to the Seine across a 100-mile front. Soon Patton was poised,
on the Seine's eastern bank, either to double back and help catch the
German forces who had survived the early August bloodbath or to go
on ahead of the Germans *before* they got to the Lorraine and find safety within a largely undefended Siegfried Line. In any case, he was at
least ready to go down the eastern bank of the Seine and pick off German divisions as they fled Normandy. Patton speculated on the possible results if he were given the green light: "I felt at this time that the
great chance of winning the war would be to let the Third Army move
with three corps, two up and one back, to the line Metz–Nancy–Epi-
nal."[21] Once he barred the line of German retreat, he would rip unmo-
lested through the empty Lorraine into an unprotected Germany itself.

Yet shortly later, the German Seventh Army and Fifth Panzer
Army, with 75,000 men and 250 tanks, were somehow allowed to cross
the Seine and head eastward, while an exasperated Patton was forced

to beg his superiors for the right to press on. He had wanted to trap the Germans on the *east* bank of the Seine, encircling them as they emerged from the river. Instead, the Allied leadership crafted a more timid strategy of intercepting them on the *west* bank, which more or less failed. "Marveling at the absence of insight among his bosses," Martin Blumenson noted, "Patton regretted their failure to let him reinforce the 79th division across the Seine. A substantial force plowing down the right bank of the river would have dealt the Germans a lethal blow. Montgomery and Bradley were uninterested, and Eisenhower, as usual, was keeping his hands off." A record of a conversation between Bradley and Patton records the latter's aggravation:

> About ten minutes after our arrival General B. [Bradley] arrived and he immediately launched into the fact that they had a big conference and decided that the Third Army shouldn't go beyond . . . Dreux . . . and Chartres. . . and toward the Seine . . . so as to leave an escape route for the Germans in the Falaise pocket. After Gen. B. had informed Gen. P. [Patton] [that he] was not to advance any further and that was that, Gen. P. told Gen. B. that since he was already to the Seine River, in fact had pissed in the river that morning and had just come from there, what would he want him to do—pull back. . . ? After much discussion Gen. B. told him how strong the people [Germans] were in the Falaise pocket and didn't think Gen. P. would be able to contain them, and it was his orders to leave an escape route to the east for them.[22]

As a consequence of that failure of nerve, when Patton was denied gasoline ten days later in the Lorraine, there were German troops aplenty nearby to reconstitute a defense. Had he pressed on at top speed from the Seine, or at least been allowed to sweep along the eastern shore of the river to catch retreating German armies, German divisions would still have found themselves surrounded when his supplies were later cut off. Patton himself wrote on August 20 of the constant temptation to act conservatively—a sense of fear that he had long since mastered:

> I always have a funny reaction before a show like this. I think of the plan and am all for it, and then just as I give the order, I get nervous and must say to myself, "Don't take counsel of your fears," and then go ahead. It is like a steeplechase—you want to ride in it, and then when the saddling bugle goes, you are scared, but when the flag is dropped all is well.[23]

Patton and his army had an incredible August, maintaining a drive that had terrified the previously formidable Germans and demoralized almost all formal opposition. The Third Army had advanced over 400 miles in 26 days, liberating 47,829 square miles of French territory in less than a month. It had killed over 16,000 Germans, wounded 55,000, and captured 65,000—and was now poised on the east bank of the Seine to stop any Germans from retreating eastward across the river. A shell-shocked and defeated German army was in full retreat, heading through the Lorraine to make a last ditch stand on the Rhine. However, with the subsequent exhaustion of Patton's supplies—due to unnecessary adherence to Eisenhower's broad front strategy, logistical incompetence, and support for Montgomery's ill-conceived Arnheim offensive—Third Army suddenly ground to a halt. From August 29 until mid-September, it scarcely advanced eastward. German generals called this reprieve "the Miracle of the West," and later admitted that there had been little organized resistance in front of Patton for most of late August and early September, due to the shock of the Third Army's speed and of its propensity to outflank and trap a succession of German divisions.[24]

Patton's desperate entreaties to sprint across Germany, before enemy units could reform, were couched to Eisenhower and Bradley in language reflecting his zeal to eliminate the German army as quickly as possible and shorten the war. Of Eisenhower's inability to grasp the "unforgiving minute," and his blinkered adherence to traditional tactics of big battles, Patton wrote: "He kept talking about the future great battle of Germany, while we assured him that the Germans have nothing left to fight with if we push on now. If we wait, there will be a great battle of Germany." In Patton's eyes, Eisenhower's worries over protocol and adherence to traditional tactical doctrine simply spelled death for thousands. In a rare moment of candor, without his usual antics, Patton confessed, at a September 7 press conference, his desire to avoid killing by collapsing armies from the rear: "If we hit opposition, we try not to boot into it. We try to hold and go around and then have the infantry clean it out. That is quite a nuisance, but we make time that way. If we stopped to wipe out these people, we would be back at the Seine now."[25]

With Patton's halt came a general stasis. Bradley later claimed that there was no real chance for Patton to cross the Rhine, and again denigrated Patton's flair and his adoption of the indirect approach.

> Undeniably Patton had a marvelous talent for gaining ground—and headlines. Without meaning to detract from his extraordinary achievements, Patton's great and dramatic gains, beginning in Sicily and continuing through Brittany and on across the Seine at Mantes, Melun and Troyes, had been made against little or no opposition. Until now Patton had not really had a serious fight on his hands, and I was certain that sooner or later Patton was going to have one. I was not sure how good a tactician he would be in a tough fight. None of his divisions had ever been put to the real test.[26]

The Lorraine was not cleared in late August. That took another sixteen weeks and thousands of American dead, as defeated and demoralized Germans reformed and entrenched across the Rhine. Patton noted that the cutoff of supplies had occurred on the twenty-

ninth of August, "one of the critical days of the war," and pondering
the French landscape, dotted with monuments to the World War I
dead, he added: "I could not help but think our delay in pushing
forward would probably result, after due course of time, in the erec-
tion of many other monuments for men who, had we gone faster,
would have lived."[27]

Postwar assessments agreed with Patton's bleak conclusions.
The British historian Ian Hogg lamented, "There can be little doubt
that Eisenhower's decision was wrong in every particular, and if
Patton had been given his supplies, and his head, there is every like-
lihood that the war could have been shortened by six months. It is a
matter of record that two-thirds of all the Allied casualties in Europe
were suffered after the September check." Hubert Essame added,
"Providence had given Eisenhower the greatest cavalry leader and
as good an army as his country had ever produced: at the decisive
moment he failed to use them."[28]

A final and equally tragic mistake occurred during Christmas 1945,
on the eve of the Battle of the Bulge, when the supposedly reckless
Patton, alone of the American commanders, sensed danger: "First Army
is making a terrible mistake in leaving the VIII Corps static. It is highly
probable that the Germans are building up east of them." And when
the Germans did hit directly the VIII Corps of the First Army, Patton
alone called for an immediate attack to the enemy column's rear—a
large enveloping maneuver that might well have cut off the entire source
of support for a quarter of a million men. Patton preferred to slam into
the vacuum to the south, in the German lines left by the Rundstedt
advance, or barring that, to cut the bulge off at its base rather than
pushing back its head. For such a subtle and intricate plan of maneuver, Patton nevertheless adopted the standard language of blood and
guts: "Hell, let's have the guts to let the sons of bitches go all the way
to Paris. Then we'll really cut 'em up and chew 'em up."[29]

Eisenhower brushed Patton's advice aside, preferring a head-
on slugfest to strike the acme of the offensive: "We discussed the
advisability of attempting to organize a simultaneous attack some-

what farther to the west, against a southern shoulder of the salient. It was concluded that future events might indicate the desirability of such a move, but that for the moment we should, in that locality, merely insure the safety of the shoulder and confine our attacks to the sector indicated." Notice the anonymous language of bureaucratese used to describe human decisions that cost thousands of American lives: "we discussed the advisability of attempting to organize"; "It was concluded that future events might indicate the desirability of"; and "to the sector indicated."[30]

Patton earlier had predicted Eisenhower's response: "That's too daring for them. My guess is that our offensive will be called off and we will have to go up there and save their hides." When Patton then offered to redirect his army's advance to the Bulge with three divisions in forty-eight hours, Eisenhower once more scoffed: "Don't be fatuous, George." In fact, it was Eisenhower who was fatuous, since Patton did attack within forty-eight hours, addressing his departing columns in the following words: "Everyone in this army must understand that we are not fighting this battle in any half-cocked manner. It's either root hog—or die! Shoot the works. If those Hun bastards want war in the raw then that's the way we'll give it to them!" Yet, once again, for all his bloody theatrics, Patton all along had preferred to envelop, not assault, the entire German offensive—"not kicking a monkey in his face" when you could "cut his tail." As his aide Charles Codman remarked, "Patton would have liked to have seen the Germans drive some forty or fifty miles, then chop them off and destroy them, but he recognized that he would never muster support for that kind of daring."[31]

Failure to adopt Patton's plans for either a small or extensive envelopment at the Battle of the Bulge proved deadly to thousands of American soldiers. Trevor Dupuy, historian of the battle, puts the missed opportunity into proper human terms.

It is hard to understand why this concept of using the relatively fresh and victorious XII Corps to cut off the German spearheads was not accepted. Bold, yes. Risky, possibly.

Foolhardy, no. Had this been done, about fifteen German divisions, including most of the best armored divisions left in the German Army, might have been cut off, and it is hard to see how, even in speculation, they could have avoided destruction. Had this occurred, the Battle of the Bulge would have ended two weeks earlier than it eventually did, thousands of American and German lives would have been saved, and the war probably would have ended in February or March, instead of May, saving many thousands more German, British, American, and Russian lives.[32]

Patton the Humanist?

What, then, are we to make of George Patton? As critics have argued, his slurs and bombast might have been symptomatic of brain damage from numerous concussions. Or he may have been an exhausted man of sixty, whose age and the hectic summer of 1944 explain much of his postwar departure from accepted norms of behavior. He was surely aristocratic by birth, and felt that the privilege of speaking his mind was a birthright that he had re-earned many times over. All that and more can explain his outbursts. But, just as likely, George Patton—who was known to create warlike faces in the mirror to capture the proper killing-look of a traditional general, and who sought to lower his squeaky voice—cultivated the appearance of a bloodthirsty conqueror. By the orthodoxy of the Western infantry tradition, he was fighting a very different type of war, in which destroying the enemy on the battlefield was relatively less important than destroying communications, capturing entire armies, and racing through an enemy's fatherland to end a war.

It remains to us to ask who, in the end, are the humanists? In this regard, Patton invites comparison with popular American icons such as Bradley and Eisenhower, both of whom were good men. Yet neither saw battle in World War I, in which Patton was nearly killed.

At one time or another, both were Patton's juniors in rank and learned much of what they understood about Blitzkrieg from Patton. Both were soft-spoken and appeared erudite in public; neither was as well-read or as intellectually curious as Patton. The two often talked of the welfare of the GI and the need to avoid needless casualties—even as their traditional conservatism lost numerous opportunities to use American forces in dramatic advances that would have alone saved American lives. In meetings, a vulgar Patton screamed about the need for advance, the necessity of bringing divisions up to full strength, and the horrendous inefficiencies of the American logistical system. A gentlemanly Bradley, he complained bitterly, kept quiet for fear of offending his superiors: "As usual Bradley said nothing. He does all the getting along and does it to his own advantage. I expect I take a chance because at heart the army is not my living and besides, I am a soldier, a simple soldier."[33]

Patton was as duplicitous and hungry for glory as any American general—indeed more so. Nevertheless, his point of being a simple soldier rang true: Eisenhower's career would be preparatory for politics, Bradley's for further promotion within the military hierarchy. Patton was older and of independent means. Had he lived much beyond the armistice, he would have neither wished nor found further career advancement or the political spotlight. He scoffed at feelers of political office, and expressed a desire to write and travel amid a comfortably aristocratic existence. Like Sherman, whom he quoted in these matters, the capital of his victories would not be transferable outside the sphere of military operations. Since Patton's energy was directed solely to advancing the Third Army as quickly as possible against the enemy in the field—often in a manner that would bother both Americans at home and superiors abroad—he really did remain a simple soldier who would gain the greatest respect among the GIs whom he led, former German adversaries whom he fought, and military historians whom he impressed as neither Eisenhower nor Bradley ever could.

Should we sympathize with the efforts of Eisenhower and Brad-ley, who had political responsibilities beyond the battlefield, to bridle Patton and his grandiose plans to determine the nature of the Allied advance to the Rhine? It is difficult to see how, when the lives of hun-dreds of thousands of soldiers, and millions of innocents in the death camps, were at stake. Scholars today argue over who allowed the Fal-aise Gap to stay open, not whether it was wise to leave it open. They debate whether closing it would have ended outright the war in the West, not whether it would have proved inconsequential. In all such speculations, Patton alone is *not* blamed.

From what we know of German defenses in the Lorraine in late August and of the success of American tactical air forces, it is hard to see how a supplied Patton would have been destroyed crossing the Rhine in late summer 1944; controversy remains only over how far Patton could have advanced into Germany without being eventual-ly surrounded. We know, of course, the horror that continued in the death camps from September 1944 to May 1945. The Germans them-selves thought that Patton's idea to cut the Bulge off at its base was the preferred course of action; no serious American historian dis-agrees, and none blame Patton for the safe retreat of the Panzers to the Rhine.

Who knows what a proconsul Patton would have done in an occupied Germany in late 1944? Eisenhower might have lost his chance to become president when faced with relieving the hero of Falaise, Brest, the Seine, Lorraine, and the liberator of Prague. Can we imagine Patton press releases after bagging an entire German army at Falaise, in little more than a week after taking command? If his superiors' opposition failed to muzzle him, how might their full sup-port and his continual victories have affected his rhetoric? Might not British historians today still decry a canceled Market-Garden, claim-ing that had Montgomery had Patton's supplies, he too would have reached Germany in 1944? As victor of Normandy, of course, Patton would have been insufferable, and like Sherman he would have been criticized—but probably not relieved—in a postwar Germany.

But these are mostly questions of protocol and politics, not military questions that involved the lives of thousands of young men. Quite simply, there were few "what ifs" involved with Montgomery, Bradley, or Hodges, because they either did not create situations which could have changed the course of the war, or if they did on rare occasions—such as Market-Garden and the crossing at Remagen—they were given full material and command support from their superiors. With all other generals in France except Patton, there was usually the criticism that material supplies—in the hedgerows, at Arnheim, at the Rhine—were not wisely used, not that they were not given.

At a time when the American army of George Marshall was wonderfully organized, trained, and equipped in the image of the modern bureaucratic state, Eisenhower and Bradley were exemplars of the best that such an order might produce—sound technicians whose errors might not cost their nation a war. Patton, in contrast, stood in antithesis to the system in which he operated, not because he deliberately wished to be contradictory, but because he saw the dangers inherent in a bureaucracy in which men were secondary to machines, individuals to an organization, originality to uniformity. Patton wished to win a war more quickly and economically than his resources justified, while his superiors wished not to lose it as their supplies and manpower increased.

America was horrified at Patton's brutal and misguided slapping of two American soldiers, but it said little when Bradley and Eisenhower stopped Patton's drives at Argentan, the Seine, in Brittany, at the Lorraine, and before the Rhine—decisions that resulted not in public embarrassment and the humiliation of a few, but in thousands of casualties in a war that should have been over. The real brutality in war is not uncouth speech, profanity, or even slurs that are racist or sexist, but rather manners and protocol that serve to hide timidity and begrudge talent. The former hurts our feelings; the latter costs us our sons' lives. Had Patton been given freer command, thousands more Americans would have come back from Europe, not because their general was a reasonable or sympathetic man—he often was neither—

but because he had mastered the art of mechanized warfare and understood the critical relationship between speed and salvation in modern battle like no other American of his generation. He was not wedded to the idea of advancing along a broad front, of engaging Germans in a series of set battles, or of securing flanks before charging ahead. His tragedy is not merely that he was a flawed character, misquoted, or even misunderstood, but that his rhetorical excesses and murderous approaches to fighting were never seen in their rightful context, as the proper and critical counterweight to waging a humanitarian way of war—to defeating the enemy without assaulting him head-on, thus without incurring as many casualties in victory as in defeat. Along with William Tecumseh Sherman, George S. Patton remains the most misunderstood and underappreciated general in United States military history.

Notes

1. For a sampling of the hatred shown Patton, see C. D'Este, *Patton. A Genius for War* (New York: HarperCollins, Publishers, 1995), pp. 812–13.
2. S. L. A. Marshall's comments: cf. D'Este, *Patton*, p. 815; C. Whiting, *Patton's Last Battle* (Briarcliff Manor, NY: Stein Day, 1987), p. 22; Bradley's criticisms are found in O. Bradley and C. Blair, *A General's Life. An Autobiography by General of the Army* (New York: Simon & Schuster, 1983), p. 464. For other criticism of Patton's indirect approach, see R. Weigley, *Eisenhower's Lieutenants* (Bloomington, IN: Indiana University Press, 1981), pp. 244–45.
3. M. Blumenson, *The Patton Papers. 1940–1945* (Boston: Houghton Mifflin, 1957; 1972), p. 524.
4. See V. Hanson, *Carnage and Culture: Landmark Battles in the Rise of Western Power* (New York: Doubleday, 2001), pp. 21–24; *The Western Way of War* (Berkeley and Los Angeles: University of California Press, 2000), pp. 8–18.
5. Herodotus 7.9.2
6. Curtius, Alexander 4.13.23; Plutarch, Alexander 32.3–4.
7. Hanson, *Carnage and Culture*, pp. 250–53, 324–33.
8. Varro at Cannae: Livy 22.61; Greek generals: Hanson, *Western Way of War*, pp. 113–14.
9. Worries that Patton was at odds with traditional American emphasis on frontal assault: V. Hanson, *The Soul of Battle* (New York: Free Press, 1999), pp. 268–96.
10. B. H. L. Liddell Hart, *Strategy. The Indirect Approach* (London, New York: Praeger, Inc., 1954), pp. 24–25. Cf. 352, "For more than a century the prime canon of military doctrine has been that 'the destruction of the enemy's main forces on

the battlefield' constituted the only true aim in war. That was universally accepted, engraved in all military manuals, and taught in staff colleges."

11. See Hanson, *Soul of Battle*, pp. 52–61.

12. For Sherman's rhetoric, criticisms directed against his failure to engage the enemy in decisive battles, and the degree of damage inflicted in Georgia, see Hanson, *Soul of Battle*, pp. 221–30, 232–35.

13. D'Este, *Patton*, p. 623.

14. Blumenson, *Patton Papers, II*, p. 458.

15. Ibid., p. 841.

16. For Patton's and Bradley's comments, see M. Blumenson, *The Battle of the Generals* (New York: Morrow, 1993), pp. 210–11; *Patton Papers, II*, p. 598; C. D'Este, *Decision in Normandy* (New York: Dutton, 1988), pp. 429–32; Weigley, *Eisenhower's Lieutenants*, pp. 208–11; E. Florentin, *The Battle of the Falaise Gap* (New York: Hawthorne Books, 1967), p. 118. Cf. S. Ambrose, *Citizen Soldiers* (New York: Simon & Schuster, 1997), p. 89, on what Patton envisioned:

> He had trained and equipped Third Army for just this moment. Straight east to Paris, then northwest along the Seine to seize the crossings, and the Allies would complete an encirclement that would lead to a bag of prisoners bigger than North Africa or Stalingrad. More important, it would leave the Germans defenseless in the west, because Patton could cut off the German divisions in northern France, Belgium, and Holland as he drove for the Rhine.

17. *Patton Papers* II, p. 508–9.

18. Bradley's objections: Bradley, *General's Life*, pp. 298–99.

19. H. Essame, *Patton: The Commander* (London, 1974), p. 172.

20. Cf. the similar assessment of Martin Blumenson, *Generals*, pp. 22–23:

> The fact was, the Allies had the Germans on the ropes in Normandy and had been unable to administer the knockout blow. As the exhilaration of the moment vanished, optimistic intelligence reports foretelling the imminent collapse of Germany quickly changed in tone and substance. . . . Large operations of encirclement are extremely difficult to execute, but the Allies let the chance for the overwhelming victory slip through their fingers. What should have been a finely tuned and well-oiled maneuver was inept and bumbled, displaying contradictory impulses. Hesitation, wrangling, and uncertainty marred the venture. The Germans themselves had foolishly pushed their heads into a noose, and the Allies had been unable to pull the string shut. They closed the Falaise pocket too slowly and then failed to trap the fleeing Germans at the Seine.

21. Report on meeting between Bradley and Patton: Blumenson, *Patton Papers, II*, 521–22. Patton's disappointment about the stop at the Seine: G.S. Patton, *War as I Knew It* (Boston: Houghton Mifflin, [1947] 1975), p. 88.

22. Martin Blumenson's assessment: Blumenson, *Generals*, pp. 253, cf. 257:

> What the Germans feared was an immediate and ruthless drive down the right bank of the river, as Patton had wished to initiate. Such an advance would have completely destroyed the German armies that had fought in Normandy. Further resistance in France would have been futile. The path to Germany would have been undefended and open to the invading Al-

lied forces. The Germans were unable to fathom why the Allies failed to pursue this course of action. After the war, Eberbach said, "I still don't understand why the Allies did not crush us at the Seine."

23. Patton, *War As I Knew It*, p. 87.

24. Statistics on Third Army progress: L. Farago, *Patton. Ordeal and Triumph* (New York: I. Oblensky, 1964), pp. 458–59.

25. Blumenson, *Patton Papers, II*, pp. 537, 543.

26. Bradley, *General's Life*, p. 317.

27. Patton, *War As I Knew It*, p. 94.

28. For Patton's assessments about his fuel being curtailed, see Blumenson, *Patton Papers, II*, pp. 523, 531; Patton, *War*, pp. 94, cf. 92, 108–9. Patton's halt, see Essame, *Patton*, 201–2; I. Hogg, *Patton* (Greenwich, CT: Bison Books, 1983), p. 115. On August 30, Patton wrote in his diary:

    We must get a crossing on the Meuse. In the last war I drained 3/4 of my tanks to keep the other 1/4 going. Eddy can do the same. It is terrible to halt, even on the Meuse. We should cross the Rhine in the vicinity of Worms, and the faster we do it, the less lives and munitions it will take. No one realizes the terrible value of the "unforgiving minute" except me. Some way I will get on yet. (Blumenson, *Patton Papers, II*, p. 531).

29. Patton's comments in general about the Battle of the Bulge: D'Este, *Patton*, pp. 678–81; Blumenson, *Patton Papers, II*, pp. 599–600. On the numbers involved in the battle: Dupuy, *Hitler's Last Gamble* (New York: Schocken Books, [1967] 1994), pp. 16–19. For Patton's anticipation of the German attack, see Weigley, *Eisenhower's Lieutenants*, pp. 498-99. General Von Rundstedt called the American avoidance of the shoulders of the bulge the "small solution"; cf. Dupuy, *Hitler's Last Gamble*, pp. 32, 365–66, cf. 210. For Patton's bombastic remarks at Verdun, see Eisenhower, *Crusade in Europe* (New York: Doubleday, 1948), p. 350; Bradley, *General's Life*, pp. 358–59.

30. Eisenhower's remarks at Verdun: Eisenhower, *Crusade in Europe*, p. 350, and his bureaucratese, p. 352.

31. Eisenhower's address to his soldiers and comments of the monkey's tail: D'Este, *Patton*, p. 683; Weigley, *Eisenhower's Lieutenants*, p. 566; cf. Patton, *War*, pp. 168–75. On the Allied plans of response, the tardy nature of Montgomery's attack, and the general opposition to Patton's more dramatic suggestions of retaliation, see Weigley, *Eisenhower's Lieutenants*, pp. 546–47. Codman's remarks: D'Este, *Patton*, p. 61. On the general failure of the Allied leadership to lop off the German salient, see J. Morelock, *General of the Ardennes. American Leadership in the Battle of the Bulge* (Washington, DC: National Defense University Press, 1994), pp. 76–80.

32. Dupuy, *Hitler's Last Gamble*, p. 210.

33. Blumenson, *Patton Papers*, II, p. 434.

STORM LANDINGS:
TARAWA TO KYUSHU

JOSEPH H. ALEXANDER

"Few missiles or weapons have ever spread such flaming terror, such scorching burns, or such searing death."[1] These words, which sound hauntingly like those we heard and read following the terrorist attacks in New York and Washington, were written fifty years ago by the great naval historian Samuel Eliot Morison. He was writing about "the kamikaze in their self destroying onslaughts," the suicide attacks the Japanese had launched against the U.S. Fifth Fleet near Okinawa in the spring and summer of 1945. These kamikazes were trying desperately to stem the tide of storm landings that were bringing the war closer and closer to their homeland.

The Japanese used the expression "storm landings" to describe, with some concern, the new American offensive strategy in the Pacific, which was to surround Japan's fortified island outposts, pound them with naval gunfire and carrier-based aviation, and then launch full frontal assaults against their fortifications and defending garrisons in broad daylight. Having gained a foothold, U.S. forces could maintain the momentum to steamroll the defenders of the islands into oblivion. Storm landings caused the Japanese considerable concern for several reasons. One was simple confusion. This was not the way the Japanese had conducted their amphibious operations when they had been

101

on the offensive in the Pacific. Lacking the size, scope, and scale of U.S. amphibious capabilities in the late years of the Pacific War, the Japanese had always landed small units at night, and almost always against a long undefended stretch of coastline, such as in China, the Kra peninsula of Malaya, and Borneo. Such tactics, of course, were applied in larger scale, but along the same principles, by General Douglas MacArthur in his fifty-six amphibious landings in New Guinea. In the Central Pacific, with its vast ocean areas and tiny islands fortified to the teeth, this would not be the case.

Seven U.S. operations qualify as "storm landings" using the operational definition of risky, large-scale, long-range assaults from the sea against heavily fortified island positions. All occurred in the Central Pacific Theater: Tarawa in the Gilbert Islands; Saipan, Guam, and Tinian in the Marianas; Peleliu in the Palau Islands; Iwo Jima in the Volcano Islands; and Okinawa in the Ryukyu Islands. The eighth would have been the island of Kyushu, the southernmost home island of imperial Japan.

Storm landings were joint operations that elicited an unusually high level of cooperation among the various services. Eleven U.S. divisions made these seven landings: six Marine, five Army. The Marines were trained, organized, and equipped for amphibious operations, and they fought their way ashore as the spearhead in each storm landing. The Army provided the larger numbers and the heavier staying power that made the landings work. Army divisions landed alongside the Marines at Guam and Okinawa.

The Navy delivered these forces ashore, but they were much more than a seaborne taxi service. Each storm landing required the Navy to "kick open the door." To *storm* across the beaches, the troops had to be delivered with their full unit integrity intact. The first squad of the first platoon of the first company of the first battalion had to land on a specific sector of the beach with the adjoining units arrayed according to plan. This is why opposed amphibious landings are the most difficult of all military operations.

To enable these storm landings to succeed, the Navy also had to establish and maintain command of the seas. To achieve this control, it fought three tremendous sea battles during the time of these landings: the Battle of the Philippines Sea in July 1944; the Battle of Leyte Gulf in October 1944; and the Battle of the East China Sea in 1945. By holding control of the seas, the U.S. could cut the flow of supplies and reinforcements to Japan's island outposts. The U.S. Army Air Forces also contributed mightily, with their tactical long-range bombing program.

There were two theaters, and two theater commanders, in the Pacific. General Douglas MacArthur, who can kindly be described as flamboyant, colorful, and imperious, commanded the Southwest Pacific theater. The Commander in Chief of the Central Pacific theater —the man responsible for the larger slice of the Pacific and the major sea battles of the war—was Fleet Admiral Chester W. Nimitz. Nimitz was the complete opposite of MacArthur. He was a quiet, reserved, private man who did not seek publicity and who, in fact, preferred to speak through members of his staff. Nimitz left no diary, kept no journal, and wrote no tell-all book at the end of the war (as did Halsey and MacArthur). Before he died, he told his wife to burn his wartime letters, and she largely complied. What is left to study, then, are some letters that Nimitz wrote to his lieutenants, fleet commanders, task force commanders, and to his direct boss—the ferocious Ernest King, Fleet Admiral, Chief of Naval Operations, Commander in Chief, U.S. Fleet, and a member of the Joint Chiefs of Staff—as well as the reminiscences of Nimitz's personal aide-de-camp and members of his staff. From these, one can draw conclusions about Nimitz's character, which sheds some light on how he conducted storm landings.

Chester Nimitz was a superb judge of character. He could assess a man's strengths and weaknesses and then employ him where he could serve best. Nimitz selected the great fleet commanders Raymond Spruance and William Halsey; the great amphibious force commander, Richmond Kelly Turner; and the colorful and long-time leader of the Marine Corps and Army landing forces, Major General Holland M. "Howling Mad" Smith. After a few false starts, Nimitz was also an uncommonly patient commander in chief. He knew how and when to stiff-arm the insistent demands for reports and updates from Admiral King back in Washington. He knew when to maintain radio silence. He let fleet commanders fight their battles, and he would wait for them to call him with assessments of their situations—win, lose, or draw. This was not an easy thing to do, and Nimitz had as difficult a time with it as anyone. There were two ways he would control his emotions as he waited for battles to unfold. If he felt confident about the outcome, he would pitch horseshoes outside his headquarters in Makalapa Heights, above Pearl Harbor. If he was concerned about an operation, as he was with Leyte and Tarawa, he would get out his target pistol and fire hundreds of rounds of .22 caliber ammunition in his small personal firing range. Nimitz's musical tastes also reflected his leadership style. He preferred symphonies or big bands, and disliked ensembles, combos, and particularly soloists. He enjoyed hearing a multitude of instruments blending together into a composite whole. And despite his pink cheeks and grandfatherly demeanor, Nimitz had the soul of a cutthroat gambler. He was not afraid to take great risks, which he did throughout the war—to the astonishment, and sometimes the horror, of his staff.

We can divide the war in the Pacific into two parts. The first begins with Pearl Harbor and continues through the landing at Bougainville in the Northern Solomons in early November 1943. This part of the war was characterized by a sharp paucity of men and materiel. The Pacific was always "Secondhand Rose" to the primary theater of Europe, but this was especially true during this early period. There weren't enough ships; there definitely weren't enough carriers; there weren't enough planes or amphibious forces. Those were desperate days, with few shining victories and some galling defeats. U.S. efforts consisted mainly in keeping the Japanese off-balance, while trying to establish some form of momentum in the offensive.

The second half of the war in the Pacific, beginning with Tarawa, was a totally different story. This was a time of plentiful resources, which grew to enormous proportions, and of huge sweeping offensives.

Nimitz, with a shorter supply line to the U.S. than MacArthur, was the first to receive these new assets, and he used them with great proficiency. The best and most effective of these was the Essex class fleet carrier, which arrived in late 1943. Not only could it carry twice as many planes, it was much faster and much more durable in combat. The arrival of dozens of these carriers would turn the tide irrevocably. Up to this point, Nimitz had been struggling to maintain his fleet and to preserve the very few carriers—sometimes just two or three—under his command. Those ships had been his crown jewels. But now he also had fast battleships that could keep up with and protect the carriers. Also coming on-line were new carrier aircraft, like the Hell Cats and the Corsairs; variable-time fuses for anti-aircraft fire; amphibious ships, like the tank-landing ship and the remarkable LSD, the dock-landing ship with a submersible well deck; and an array of high-speed logistic support ships. Nimitz now had the means to establish a new fleet, which he would eventually call the Fifth Fleet and whose command he would give to Admiral Spruance.

Nimitz realized he had the components to revolutionize naval warfare in the Pacific. However, to do this he had to overcome three obstacles. One was the naval tradition, going back to Lord Nelson, that "a ship is a fool to fight a fort," that is, that we had no business sending warships against the huge coastal defense guns of the Japanese. The second obstacle was MacArthur's dictum, also held by some on Nimitz's staff, that amphibious operations were too risky unless conducted within range of land-based aviation. The third obstacle was the naval belief, also held by of some Nimitz's staff, that following each engagement the fleet should return to Pearl Harbor for replenishment, repair, and rearmament. Nimitz swept these notions off the board.

The first test of Nimitz's revolution in naval warfare came in the Gilbert Islands—a small scattering of coral-encrusted sand spits near the equator, about two thousand miles southwest of Pearl Harbor. The value of the Gilberts—British possessions that the Japanese had conquered right after Pearl Harbor—was the fine bomber strip that the Japanese had constructed on Betio Island in Tarawa Atoll. This strip had been built in reaction to the spectacular raid by Evans Carlson on Makin Atoll in August 1942. The Japanese imperial general headquarters, alarmed by this raid, realized that their backwater outposts in the Central Pacific were now vulnerable. They spent the next fifteen months building up the small island of Betio, which was no more than two-and-one-half miles long by one-half mile wide. Here they built the bomber strip and provided it with lavish defenses against attack from the sea. The small island had five hundred pillboxes and countless numbers of heavy weapons edging its perimeter. Some observers called Betio the Gibralter of the Pacific. Its commander vowed that it would take a million Americans one hundred years to capture it, and he probably believed it.

The first U.S. target in the Central Pacific should have been the Marshall Islands, but we weren't ready for them. We didn't know much about them and had to have, if nothing else, aerial photographs prior to assailing them from the sea. That is where Betio came in. At the time, the enormous cameras needed to take aerial photographs could only be carried in B-24 bombers, which could not take off from a carrier. In order to take photographs of the Marshalls, then, we needed a bomber strip within B-24 range—which the Betio bomber strip was.

Nimitz knew from the start that this amphibious assault wouldn't be easy. To this point, our landings at Guadalcanal and Tulagi had been unopposed. Smaller landings had been opposed, but they were not on the scale of Tarawa. The Gilberts were defended by a regiment of Rikusentai—the Japanese special naval landing forces, or, as some people called them, the Japanese marines. These were well-trained, well-armed, physically fit sailors from Yokosuka and Sasebo, proficient both with infantry weapons and with the large naval guns that had been dismounted and moved to parapets on shore. They were commanded by Rear Admiral Keiji Shibasaki, and they had everything they needed to fight a protracted battle against the invading Americans.

Nimitz also worried about the Japanese Combined Fleet, still very much a force, which was located not too far away, on Truk in the Eastern Carolines. He also was battling the clock. Some of the assets he was using in this new fleet had been borrowed from the European theater, following the decision not to launch a cross-Channel assault in 1943. Therefore, the Betio landing was scheduled for late November, six weeks before we would have to be fighting our way ashore in the Marshalls. There would be no time to wait for the high tide at Tarawa. There would be no time to conduct a diversionary landing, or to seize outlying islands on which to place artillery for prebombardments that could reduce the island's defenses. Nimitz's instructions to Spruance were curt: Get the hell in and get the hell out.

There were other problems at Tarawa. The Japanese had mined all of the approaches except for a small cut through the lagoon. A coral reef protected the island, as protected most other islands in the Central Pacific. Although we had plenty of Higgins boats—forty-man assault landing craft that Andrew Jackson Higgins had developed in New Orleans, and that some say won the war—they could only go over the reef at high tide, and we would be hitting Tarawa at low tide.

The plan was to attack during the rising portion of the tide, but it was still a gamble. So we converted our logistics vehicles—tracked landing vehicles—into assault vehicles. We took pig iron, scrap iron, bolted it onto the cabs of the vehicles and festooned the vehicles with machine guns. This experiment worked. We had over eighty-seven of these converted assault vehicles in the first three assault waves, and most survived both the reef and enemy fire. But the ship-to-shore assault was so long and involved that the vehicles ran out of gas as they returned to the reef to pick up the remaining Marines in their boats. Most were then shot at and blown up.

Other things went wrong. Every time our flagship, the battleship USS *Maryland*, fired her 14-inch guns, her radios would be knocked out and communications lost for an hour. The landing force radios were not waterproofed, so most failed almost immediately. For the first twenty-four hours, the main connection between the Landing Force Commander ashore, Colonel David Shoup, and his Commanding General at sea, Julian C. Smith, was a single telegraph key—and that didn't work consistently.

And then there was the tide. It failed to rise the four-and-one-half to five feet predicted by the tide tables. In fact, it didn't rise more than six inches over the next thirty hours, which was a mystery—and a tragedy. About ten years ago, a physicist in Texas discovered that when the moon is at its farthest point from the earth and that event coincides with a neap tide, the tidal fluctuations are dramatically curtailed. This is a rare occurrence, and it happened only twice in all of 1943. Once was the morning of D-Day at Tarawa. For that reason, no boat got over that reef in the first thirty hours. Every single Marine had to wade ashore through the lagoon. In photos and documentary films, you can see hundreds of them wading with their rifles over their heads, leaning forward into the fire, machine gun bullets whipping up the lagoon around them, the green waters turning red with blood. Hundreds of lives were lost as a result.

"Issue in doubt" is a term that the Marines used twice in situation reports during all of World War II. The first was at Wake Island in December 1941, as the Japanese came ashore; the second was the afternoon of D-Day at Tarawa, 20 November 1943. Neither was an exaggeration. We could easily have lost the battle that first night in Tarawa. Five thousand Marines had crossed the reef by nightfall; fifteen hundred were dead or badly wounded. Many straggled in without their weapons. They were disorganized, with pockets of men scattered up and down the beach, forming a very thin line.

Admiral Shibasaki, a veteran amphibious assault officer, knew the problems of disorganization that a landing force would suffer, particularly on the first night. He planned to assemble his forces in one flank on the east, where the Japanese had at least one thousand troops who had not been touched. They had sufficient forces, tanks, and flamethrowers to sweep up that flank with ease, capture or kill Colonel Shoup, and throw the entire landing force back into the sea. All who spent that first night on the beach believed that they were in grave danger. But nothing happened. There were no counterattacks that night—or the next. There were none until the third night. That attack was ferocious, but by then fifteen thousand Marines had come ashore, and we prevailed.

For years it was believed that Admiral Shibasaki had lost his communications and was unable to organize an attack. Many said he died on the third day of the battle—indeed, that he was the last man to die. However, that was not the case. According to Japanese accounts, Shibasaki died the first afternoon, at about the same time that General Smith reported "Issue in Doubt." Having given over his two-story concrete command post bunker (which is still standing) to serve as a hospital for his wounded troops, Shibasaki was moving his staff across the runway to an alternate post. A sharp-eyed American forward observer, seeing troops in the open, immediately notified two destroyers in the lagoon. The destroyers fired at least forty rounds, killing the Admiral and his entire staff. There was no counterattack on the first night because there was no one alive to coordinate it. On the third night, a brave lieutenant pulled together an attack, but it was too late. The Japanese chose not to surrender and fought to the death. Those who survived committed suicide. Only six Rikusentai and several dozen laborers were captured.

In the immediate aftermath of Tarawa, the commanders involved sorted out what had worked and what had not. Thus, six weeks later in the Marshall Islands, a number of the problems had been corrected. Underwater demolition teams guided the troops through the reefs and searched for obstacles and mines. There was a dedicated amphibious force command ship with its own communication suites. The landing force had waterproof radios, many more flamethrowers, and landing vehicle tracks. It was impressive that such improvements were realized in just six weeks. Even more important, Tarawa validated the controversial new doctrine of offensive amphibious assaults against heavily fortified, strongly defended islands. If it worked at Tarawa, under the worst possible tactical and hydrographic conditions, it could work anywhere. It could work at Saipan and Iwo Jima. It could work at Normandy.

The abiding image of Tarawa, however, is the carnage. One of every three Marines who was hit by gunfire died, which reflects the point-blank range and the high velocity weapons involved. At the end of the three-day fight, there was a total of six thousand dead—five thousand Japanese, one thousand Americans—on that small island.

The Pacific War turned a significant corner at Tarawa. Admiral Spruance captured the Gilbert Islands in two weeks time. The successful campaign relieved the Joint Chiefs of Staff, who had gambled to support Nimitz's proposals. Now they endorsed his plans for the subsequent invasion of the Marshalls—and even the Marianas, advancing a thousand miles closer to Japan.

During the Marianas campaign, on July 21, 1944, we liberated Guam, which had been a U.S. possession since 1898. (The island still celebrates July 21 as their liberation day.) This was an especially sweet victory for the Marines, who established their camp on the ruins of their old barracks. Elsewhere in the Marianas, we seized Saipan and Tinian to enhance the strategic bombing campaign against Japan. The Marianas beachheads involved much larger islands, with mountains, caves, farms, and cities. Seizing them took longer, and resulted in a much higher butcher's bill—sixteen thousand at Saipan alone. But seizing the Marianas gave the U.S. invaluable bases for heavy bombers.

Tokyo realized the significance of this loss. Saipan was within Japan's absolute national defensive sphere, and Japan's leaders never imagined that it could be taken so swiftly. They knew the range of the new B-29 Super Fortresses—twelve hundred miles, twenty-four hundred miles round-trip—and they knew that at that range Tokyo was in danger. "Hell is upon us," said one member of the Royal Family. The Tojo government had to resign in disgrace after this series of defeats in the Marianas.

The Japanese, however, learned from these catastrophes. They studied the storm landings and decided to modify their doctrine for island defense. No longer would they defend at the water's edge; no longer would they waste their remaining assets on glorious but ineffective banzai attacks that would result in the deaths of the defenders. Instead they would preserve their assets and force the Americans into a battle of attrition, dragging out the fight and imposing extremely high numbers of casualties. This, they thought, would work on the minds of the American people and improve chances for an armistice, as in World War I. Thus Japan could avoid unconditional surrender, war crime trials, reparations, and the possible loss of their emperor. Japanese defenders of the islands were encouraged to dig in and to use cave warfare defense. They were to disrupt the landings and kill as many Americans as they could on D-Day, but not to put too many assets in the open where they would be blasted by prelanding bombardments.

The last three great storm landings of the Pacific war occurred at Peleliu, Iwo Jima, and Okinawa. Peleliu was a reversion, largely because of Japan's new tactics and partly because the U.S. was getting cocky. For example, the commanding general of the 1st Marine Division, who led the assault on Peleliu, bragged to his troops before D-Day: "This is going to be rough, but fast. We'll be out of here in three days, maybe two. Somebody bring me the Japanese commander's sword."[2] Colonel Kunio Nakagawa, who had been decorated nine times for bravery, commanded the defenders. This regiment had been pulled from the front lines of the Kwantung Army, which was defending Manchuria against the Soviet Union. Its history went back to the war with China in 1895. Nakagawa recognized, no doubt, that Peleliu was a defender's dream.

Tokyo sent in mining engineers and tunneling experts who converted existing caves into a honeycomb of interlocking defensive positions. There were five hundred caves; some could hold one thousand men, while others were just big enough for an anti-tank gun and crew. They were concentrated in a devilish piece of moonscape that the natives called the Umurbrogol, the Japanese called Momoji, and the Americans called "Bloody Nose Ridge." It proved particularly bloody for the 1st Marine Regiment, which was commanded by the colorful, unique, and legendary Colonel Lewis B. "Chesty" Puller. The 1st Marines fought for six days at Bloody Nose Ridge, losing more than half their number. One battalion lost 71 percent of its landing strength; almost all were infantrymen who carried the fight up into the ridge.

On D-Day at Peleliu, Nakagawa disrupted the landing very effectively with fire from mountain caves. One young private first-class, who kept notes in the margins of his New Testament, recorded his impressions of that day. Eugene B. Sledge went ashore in the third wave. "The beach was a sheet of flame," he wrote, "backed by a huge wall of black smoke as though the whole island was on fire. Every Marine in that amphibian tractor was sickly white with terror." Sledge made it through the battle of Peleliu untouched, and made it through Okinawa as well. He was one of ten men who had that distinction—ten men out of the two-hundred fifty who had gone ashore at Peleliu on D-Day. He wrote about his experiences in the best book that ever came out of the ranks of the infantry of any service in that war—*With the Old Breed at Peleliu and Okinawa.* ("The Old Breed" was the 1st Marine Division.) To those who would romanticize or trivialize the fighting that took place in these storm landings, a chapter of that book, titled "Of Mud and Maggots," provides an effective antidote.[3]

Iwo Jima followed in February of 1945. There, three Marine divisions faced one of the greatest commanders the Marines had ever faced. General Tadamichi Kuribayashi fought with great ingenuity and bravery. He made the Americans pay for every yard, as they landed under heavy fire and stormed their way up the volcanic peak of Suribachi. Everyone is familiar with Joe Rosenthal's epic photograph of six men raising the U.S. flag on Iwo Jima. What few know is that the flag raising took place on the fourth day, whereas the battle raged for thirty-six days. General Kuribayashi became the only Japanese commander to inflict upon the storm-landing Americans a higher number of casualties than the Japanese would suffer on defense. General Kuribayashi, however, died in the fighting.

Improved casualty-handling techniques, developed by the U.S. after Tarawa, saved many lives. At Iwo Jima, the U.S. suffered twenty-six thousand casualties; one of every five died. At Tarawa, one of every three had died. One important improvement was that Iwo Jima's field hospital had whole blood instead of plasma. Volunteers in California would donate blood one day; it would be flown to Pearl Harbor the next ; it would reach Guam the third day; and then it was sent directly to Iwo Jima. Administering this blood were a number of Navy hospital corpsmen, who were integral members of the Marine divisions. Time and again they put themselves in grave danger to rescue and treat the wounded. Of these Navy corpsmen and field surgeons, eight-hundred fifty were killed or wounded in the fight for Iwo Jima. In addition, there were twelve female Navy flight nurses who would fly from Guam and land on Iwo Jima, while it was under fire, to deliver the blood. They then helped determine which of the wounded Marines were most critical and flew with them back to the naval hospital at Guam. Many of these Marines were seventeen and eighteen years old; some, who had falsified their ages, were sixteen. In their delirium, these young men would often call for their mothers. Lieutenant Junior Grade Norma Crotty, a twenty-three-year-old nurse from Iowa, would walk up and down the aisle of the transport aircraft and take each one by the hand, telling them to "Hang on, son, just hang on." Most of these men made it, thanks to nurses like Norma Crotty.

Fittingly, one of the six Marines immortalized in the photograph of the flag raising at Suribachi—and later in the bronze statue in Arlington—was Navy corpsman John Bradley. Three of those six men were killed in the battle of Iwo Jima. Two others—including John Bradley—were wounded. (Bradley was wounded while saving the life of another Marine.) His son, James Bradley, has written a fine book called *Flags of our Fathers,* which portrays the life and death of each of these men.

Okinawa was the largest island we would assail in the Central Pacific, and the one closest to Japan, about 350 miles south of Kyushu. The Battle of Okinawa—the greatest air, land, and sea battle in history—lasted almost three months. What made Okinawa so difficult were the Japanese suicide attacks, which were not limited to the kamikazes, but encompassed a range of tactics and techniques. Japanese carrying explosives would swim and attach themselves to the hulls of ships; midget submarines, which were essentially manned torpedoes, would be launched at ships; and power boats loaded with high explosives would be rammed into ships. Then there were the sappers: Japanese would wrap themselves with satchel charges and throw themselves at Sherman tanks, killing the crews. There wasn't a tank crew in Okinawa that wasn't more afraid of the suicidal sappers than of the anti-tank guns or mines.

By this time, the Japanese had become so desperate that the Imperial Navy ordered the giant battleship *Yamato* into a suicide action. She was given enough fuel for a one-way trip from Kure to Okinawa with a funeral cortege of a few destroyers and cruisers, no air support, and no fleet support, with the mission of running ashore. She was then to use her 18.1-inch guns to blow up every ship in the anchorage, and when she ran out of ammunition, the crew was to scuttle her and fight the Americans to the death. A year or two earlier, a threat like this from such a mighty battleship would have sent terror through the amphibious task force. But in 1945 it was not a big deal. Spruance simply said to his fast carrier task force commander,

Mark Mitscher, "You take 'em." And he did. Mitscher intercepted the *Yamato* and sank her in fifteen minutes.

A greater threat came from suicide bombers. One device, the Baku bomb, was a self-guided solid-fuel rocket that was launched from the belly of a Japanese bomber with a pilot on the last ride of his life. The first such bomb that was deployed sank the destroyer USS *Abele*. While this incident rattled the U.S. fleet, the Japanese could never repeat their success. But there were a lot of frightening near-misses.

At Okinawa, the main horrifying threat—day after day, night after night—was from the kamikazes. There had been kamikaze attacks in the Philippines, and there had been one bad night involving kamikazes in Iwo Jima, but at Okinawa they came in waves, hundreds at a time. The Japanese would send non-kamikaze aircraft (probably flown by more proficient pilots) along with these waves. The non-kamikazes would divert the U.S. combat air patrol and drop bombs on the fleet while the sailors were manning their anti-aircraft guns against the suicide bombers. For example, on April 6, within the first week of the landing at Okinawa, seven hundred Japanese planes came at once: Three hundred fifty were kamikazes, the rest were bombers and fighters. Twenty-six ships were hit; six sank. The smoke from the burning and sinking U.S. ships was so black that by the end of the day, land-based aviation flying into Kadena or Yontan airfields couldn't see. Three planes crashed in the sudden darkness.

These wave attacks would come one after the other—or in a series of four or of ten—at any hour, day or night, just to keep the exhausted sailors at general quarters and wear them down. They would often come at the full moon, and Spruance called them "witches on broomsticks." Signalman First-Class Nick Floros, standing duty on a small landing ship one night, looked up and saw one right on top of him. Huge and silent, it had cut its engine and was coming in. The kamikaze flew fifteen feet over Floros' head and blew the ship next to him to kingdom come. On April 16, the destroyer USS *Lafrey* was hit twenty-two times, including six direct hits from kamikazes and four from bombs. Yet the flags kept flying and the guns kept firing, and the *Lafrey* survived. Spruance had to evacuate the flagship *Indianapolis* when she was hit by a kamikaze. Mark Mitscher had to leave the carrier *Bunker Hill,* and when he boarded the *Enterprise,* she got hit. After that, there were signs around the fleet saying "We don't want you, Mitscher, you're bad luck."

Nimitz went ashore to talk with the Tenth Army commander: "Get moving," he said. "I'm losing a ship and a half a day out here while you're still slogging forward with this attrition warfare at 50 yards a day."[4] It didn't help. Even though they called themselves "The Fleet that Came to Stay," at the end of this victorious ninety-day battle for Okinawa, the Fifth Fleet had lost thirty-four ships and 368 more were badly damaged. There were nine thousand casualties among the sailors, and half of these died, many drowned at sea. These were the worst losses that the U.S. Navy had suffered in its 225-year history. Even so, they had shot down some twenty-two hundred kamikazes.

The next landing—the last and greatest of the storm landings—would have been Kyushu, and would have been called "Operation Olympic." It was to have taken place on November 1, 1945, with fourteen U.S. divisions and both the Third and the Fifth Fleets. The Japanese had six-hundred thousand troops defending the southern part of that island, which was the exact size of the U.S. landing force. It would have been an incredibly bloody battle, and not the least because the Japanese now had six thousand dedicated kamikaze planes, as well as at least one thousand explosive-packed powerboats. According to Japanese documents, those six thousand kamikazes were to be ordered to attack troop transports. It would have been murder beyond imagination. But, the U.S. dropped the atom bombs, and the Emperor finally decided to end the slaughter. The war was over.

The seven storm landings had cost more than one-hundred thousand American casualties. Thirteen of the slain finally came home in August 2001. Their remains had been discovered on the island of

Makin, and they were reburied in Arlington National Cemetery with full military honors. They are still coming home. Where did we get such men?

Robert Sherrod, the great combat correspondent who later became editor-in-chief of the *Saturday Evening Post*, wrote at the end of the war that while America's industrial might provided the wherewithal for victory in the Pacific, "No man who ever saw Tarawa, Saipan, Iwo Jima, or Okinawa would agree that all of that steel was in the guns and bombs alone. There was steel as well in the hearts of those young men who stormed those beaches."[5]

It is to those men, of all services, living and dead, that we owe an abiding debt. All of them went through unspeakable horrors, including suicide bomb attacks, but they prevailed—and we will as well.

Notes

1. Samuel Eliot Morison, *Victory in the Pacific, 1945*, Vol. XIV in *History of U.S. Naval Operations in World War II* (Boston: Little, Brown, 1960), p. 239.
2. George McMillan, *The Old Breed: A History of the 1st Marine Division in World War II* (Washington: Infantry Journal Press, 1949), pp. 269–70.
3. Eugene B. Sledge, *With the Old Breed at Peleliu and Okinawa*, Classics of Naval Literature Edition (Annapolis, MD: Naval Institute Press, 1996), pp. 239-60. D-Day Peleliu quote from Eugene B. Sledge, "Peleliu 1944: Why Did We Go There?" *Naval Institute Proceedings* (September 1994): 72–73.
4. E. B. Potter, *Nimitz* (Annapolis, MD: Naval Institute Press, 1976), p. 375.
5. Robert Sherrod, *On to Westward: The Battles of Saipan & Iwo Jima* (New York: Duell, Sloan & Pierce, 1945), p. 14.

Reference

Joseph H. Alexander, *Storm Landings: Epic Amphibious Battles in the Central Pacific* (Annapolis, MD: Naval Institute Press, 1997).

HITLER IN THE WAR YEARS

JOHN LUKACS

Hitler was the key to Churchill becoming the savior of England and, in many ways, the savior of Western civilization. Winston Churchill was an interesting and colorful figure in British politics, but had it not been for Adolf Hitler in the 1930s, and especially in 1940 and thereafter, Churchill would be seen—with every reason—as a minor figure in the history of the world and a secondary figure in the history of Britain. But this did not happen.

Fifty or sixty years after the war, there is an enormous amount of literature about Hitler. Twice as many books have been written about him as about Churchill and Roosevelt. These, of course, include not only biographies, but all kinds of scholarly and journalistic studies. Yet one thing that is missing from 98 percent of them is a treatment of Hitler as a statesmen and a strategist.

Unfortunately, Adolf Hitler had considerable talents as a statesmen and as a strategist. One person who was profoundly aware of this was Winston Churchill, who was a visionary. He never underestimated Hitler. As early as 1930, when Hitler was a third-rate figure on the German political scene, Churchill turned to a German diplomat at a dinner in the German embassy in London, and asked him about Hitler, who, Churchill said, may cause a lot of trouble.

All through the war—not only in the crucial time of 1940, but all through the war—many of Churchill's strategic decisions were marked by his rule never to underestimate what Hitler was capable of doing. He never underestimated the bonds—the steel bonds—that Hitler had forged to unify the German people.

We ought to admit that some of the best scholarly studies about Hitler were written by German historians, even though biography is not the Germans' main suit. (The British, because of their literary tradition, are better biographers.) But there is a strange shortcoming: Most of Hitler's German biographers deal mostly with the years before 1939. Even what I consider the best biography of Hitler, that by Joachim Fest, skims over the war years: of his 1,250 pages, 950 cover the years before 1939.

In a way, this German perspective is understandable. The German perspective on Adolf Hitler is that he was a dictator and demagogue, who, in the six short years from 1933 to 1939, brought prosperity, prestige, and confidence to the Germans. But then he led them into the Second World War. It cannot be said that the Kaiser created the First World War. One can compile a list of at least six statesmen or military leaders who were mainly responsible for the events of 1914. But had there been no Hitler in 1939, there would have been no Second World War.

The Germans believe that after 1939, when Hitler made this greatest mistake, it was all downhill. That is not so. He could have won the war. He came very close to winning it in 1940. Even in 1941, and perhaps even in 1942, he still could have won. The Germans had a population, resources, and capabilities that were a fraction of those of the Allied powers, yet it still took six years to conquer them. Hitler was not entirely, but greatly, responsible for this.

After the war, there was (and there still is) a tendency to say that Hitler was mad—that he didn't know much. Some of the German generals blamed their defeats on him. There were, of course, instances when he should have listened to his generals. But there were also plenty of instances when Hitler was right and his generals were wrong.

One principal instance when he was wrong was at the crucial turning point of Stalingrad. He had insisted that the Sixth Army not break out, that it fight to the end. Unlike Churchill, Hitler did not often address his people during the war. But he did speak to the German populace after the catastrophe of Stalingrad, and he did not deny his responsibility.

Another legend that has to be dismissed is that Hitler had ordered the German armies never to retreat, to always fight to the last shell. Yet after Stalingrad, the German armies fought a remarkably successful retreat campaign. It took the German armies about thirteen months to get to Stalingrad—1941 to 1942. It took the Russian army, with its tremendous manpower and military equipment, two-and-one-half years to get from Stalingrad to Berlin. What I am trying to emphasize here is something that Winston Churchill knew in the marrow of his bones: Don't underestimate the man and don't underestimate what he is capable of doing.

Here I come perhaps to the essence of my argument, which is the essence of Hitler's statesmanship and strategy. The clue to Hitler's statemanship and strategy is something that I may sum up in two words: he was an idealist determinist. That is a particularly German tendency. He believed that ideals matter. But he exaggerated that. He believed that the superiority of ideals (of which, of course, military morale is a consequence) determines everything.

Let me give you two striking examples. In April 1940, Hitler had a conversation with Goebbels. It appears to be one of the few conversations in which Hitler was not monologizing. Goebbels said that the war was nothing but a larger repetition of what had happened in Germany ten years before. At that time, the national socialists were a small party, but they were more determined than the others because their ideals were superior.

Hitler believed that this was why the German soldier, imbued with national socialist ideals, was worth two British soldiers and four French soldiers. This was true, he believed, not simply because of German organization or German equipment, but because the German soldiers' ideals were stronger and superior. There was some truth in this, unfortunately; but fortunately, not enough. The German soldier was perhaps a match to two British, three French, or three Russian soldiers; but he was not a match to fifteen of them. I once found an amazing statement made by one of Hitler's favorite and most able generals, Field Marshal von Model, after which he committed suicide. Nearly encircled by American forces in March 1945, this field marshal told his staff to "Hold on . . . because our ideals are so superior to that of the others that it is mathematically certain that we are going to win." Mathematically certain, in March 1945!

There was some truth in what Hitler and Model thought, but not enough. The great German military writer Karl von Clausewitz wrote, "War is the continuation of politics by other means." This is a very profound observation, but with two limitations. One is that this is essentially what Clausewitz had already learned from Machiavelli. The other is that this was particularly applicable to Clausewitz's eighteenth century, with its small dynastic wars.

Hitler knew this, but he reversed it. In many ways, his politics were the continuation of war. That is, he waged politics the way he waged war. He believed that superior strength was what mattered— whence his astonishing diplomatic victories before the war. From 1933 to 1939, he lifted the German people to great heights of unity and prosperity, unlike the Communists and unlike most other dictators. His people did not have to pay for his dictatorship with hardship. Hitler brought unity, prosperity, and confidence to the Germans.

Then he marched into the Rhineland. He took over Austria. He took a slice of Czechoslovakia. Then he took the rest of Czechoslovakia. He took a slice from Lithuania. He did all this without war. (The great Bismarck had brought about the unity of Germany, but that took three wars). Hitler's statesmanlike ability was buttressed by another talent. He hadn't traveled much; he hadn't spent much time outside Germany. But he had an uncanny understanding of the weaknesses of all kinds of human beings. This was almost a sixth sense—perhaps similar to how a dog can smell fear. From 1933 to 1939, he constantly surprised his generals and supporters, who were worried by their opponents' possible reactions, by saying, "Don't worry. They're not going to do this." Yet we are very fortunate that there was one person whom he never quite understood: Winston Churchill. When it came to their duel in 1940, when they were the two principal figures in charge of destiny, Churchill understood Hitler better than Hitler understood Churchill. That alone could not bring victory; but it was a great asset.

We still have to think a fair amount about Hitler and his thinking. For example, we speak of him and of Stalin as totalitarians. But this word does not properly apply to Adolf Hitler, for many reasons. One of them is that he had the majority of his people behind him. Moreover, when we think of totalitarianism, we think of the power of the state—a police state that controls everything. This was not quite true of Hitler's Reich. When we compare it to Russia, for example, or to other dictatorships, it is amazing to note how much personal freedom and privacy still existed under this otherwise tyrannical and evil regime.

More important, totalitarianism applies to the power of the state. Hitler did not emphasize the state. To Hitler, the state was a product of the Modern Age, as indeed it was. (During the Middle Ages, the state was weak.) He often said, "I don't represent the state, I represent the folk, the people, the nation; the people came before the state and the people are going to survive the state." He said that he created a "national socialist people, not an effective state bureaucracy." "The state," he said in one of his last speeches, "is an artificial framework (*ein Zwangsform*)." The reality is the people, the German folk. This was something very modern and very dangerous: Hitler was the true populist of the twentieth century.

The word "dictator," too, does not quite apply to Hitler. He knew that he had been democratically elected: "I have the majority of my people behind me." He once said, "Every South American popinjay can be a dictator. I am not a dictator. I am more than that." This shows his belief in the people, the belief in his ideology of national socialism, beyond the limit and the necessities of traditional statecraft. These were the marks of his genius—an evil genius, but a genius nonetheless.

Fortunately, however, there was a duality in this man—in his statesmanship, in his strategy—as there is a duality in every human being. It takes a certain kind of experience in life, or a talented biographer, to point them out. In his recent biography, Roy Jenkins points out Churchill's dualities—the hedonist and the warrior—and how Churchill resolved his duality to our great benefit. When it came to duty, when it came to dedication, the warrior triumphed over the hedonist.

Hitler subordinated the state to his faith. He subordinated statecraft to ideology. He believed in that. Near the very end of the war, he said that it was unnatural, unreasonable, impossible that the Third Reich should lose, "because we represent something that is so much stronger, so much more timely, so much more revolutionary than Communists and capitalists." Yet there is ample evidence that at times, without admitting it to himself, Hitler would elevate statecraft over ideology.

The general belief that Hitler did not admit that he was losing the war—that to the very end he fanatically believed that "this cannot happen"—is nonsense. As early as November 18, 1941— before the German armies were to be pushed back before Moscow—he made a comment to General Halder that "perhaps the war will end with a draw; perhaps neither side can annihilate the enemy." He was right. Pearl Harbor and the first Russian counteroffensive before Moscow changed things. And Hitler often changed his entire strategy not on the basis of ideology, but on the basis of statecraft.

His strategy from that point on becomes what I call "Friderician," modeled after his idol Frederick the Great. Hitler knew a fair amount of history. Almost two hundred years before, Frederick the Great had been involved in a losing war against an immense and disparate coalition. What Frederick the Great did was to split the coalition: He defeated one side, and forced the others to make deals with him. Eventually he won his war.

From November 1941 on, in my opinion, Hitler subordinated almost everything for the purpose of dividing the Allies. He said that the unnatural alliance between capitalists and communists, between Anglo-Saxons and Russians, cannot last; all coalitions break up, and this was going to break up very soon. It did break up, but fortunately too late for him.

Hitler knew what the defeat at Stalingrad meant morally. When he decided six months later, after a rather successful and careful German retreat, to start another large, last offensive in Russia, which then led to the greatest tank battle hitherto known—the Battle of Kursk—he decided to attack. The language of his order to the troops was telling. " This is not just a battle," he said. "This is supposed to be a torch to the world, *Ein fanal* . . . to show what the German armies are still capable of."

When well-meaning Germans, including General Rommel, urged him to try to get together with the Allies and reach some kind of arrangement, Hitler said, and rightly, that Germany had to win a battle first, to prove its strength.

Two months after D-Day, the Germans were finally expelled from Normandy. Very rapidly, but in relatively orderly fashion, they retreated from France and Belgium. Their retreat at the end of August and September 1944 was almost as rapid as their advance into France four years earlier. But as early as September 12, when the German army was in full retreat, Hitler summoned Rommel and said that there had to be a counteroffensive. Rommel was ordered to prepare for the Battle of the Bulge, where, again, his goal was to divide the Allies—meaning this time the Americans and the British. He would go to Antwerp, militarily dividing the Americans from the British and perhaps forcing Field Marshal Montgomery to a retreat through Belgium and southern Holland, repeating Dunkirk.

Hitler also knew far more about the United States than people give him credit for. He knew that in America, particularly among some in the Republican Party, there was a rising tide—a small but rising tide—of worry about the Russians, a worry about what was going to happen after Germany was defeated. So the counteroffensive in the Ardennes, the Battle of the Bulge, was undertaken for reasons of statecraft, for political reasons.

Beginning in March 1944, Heinrich Himmler, the head of the German secret services, on several occasions attempted to get in touch with the American secret services. It could be argued that he did this to save his own skin—except that Hitler knew of Himmler's negotiations. They were not done behind Hitler's back. The most crucial example of this were the negotiations that SS General Wolff, who was partly in charge of the German armies in Italy, had with Allen Dulles in Bern, beginning as early as February 1945. They were discussing and negotiating a German surrender in Italy, with the possibility of shifting some German troops to the Russian front. Hitler actually received Wolff on the 17th of April 1945, and tacitly agreed to this. He hoped to cause trouble between the Americans and the Russians, which he indeed succeeded in doing on some occasions. Stalin, for example, knew of these negotiations and wrote a very angry dispatch to President Roosevelt just before the president's death. Again, Hitler had succeeded; again, fortunately for us and for the world, he had not succeeded enough.

The great French moralist, La Rochefoucauld wrote, "There are evil men in this world who would be less dangerous if they didn't have some virtues in them." Such is the human condition. Such was the duality of Hitler—sometimes putting ideology over statecraft, sometimes, consciously or not, putting statecraft over ideology. But there is a duality in every man and every statesman—Roosevelt, De Gaulle, Churchill, Stalin. Only their dualities were not as disastrous for them as his were for Adolf Hitler.

STALIN AND WORLD WAR II:
PLANTING THE SEEDS
OF THE COLD WAR

HERBERT ROMERSTEIN

Addressing the Fifteenth Congress of the Soviet Communist Party in 1927, Stalin painted the picture of an isolated Soviet Union, encircled by capitalist imperial powers that were planning its military destruction. To solve this problem, Stalin referred to the teachings of Lenin.

> We must not forget Lenin's statement that as regards our work of construction, very much depends upon whether we succeed in postponing war with the capitalist world, which is inevitable, but which can be postponed either until the moment when the proletarian revolution in Europe matures, or until the moment when the colonial revolutions have fully matured, or, lastly, until the moment when the capitalists come to blows over the division of the colonies.[1]

As Stalin saw it, the non-Communist world had to be split apart, the nations within it set to fighting each other, to allow the Soviet Communists to maintain and expand their power. The development of the Nazi movement in Germany presented such an opportunity. Thus from 1929 to 1935, the world Communist movement, under Moscow's direction, had a policy of opposing not the Nazis but the Social Democrats (who the Communists called "Social Fascists").

During the Twelfth Plenum of the Executive Committee of the Communist International (Comintern) in Moscow, which took place just four months before Hitler took power in Germany in January 1933, S. Gusev, an important official of the Comintern, announced that "in Germany, at the present time ... Fascism is not our chief enemy in the workers' movement, but Social Fascism."[2] In November 1932, the Communist-run German Revolutionary Trade Union Opposition organized a transport strike against the Social Democrat city government in Berlin. In an article in the magazine of the Moscow-based Red International of Labor Unions, the German Communists boasted, "This powerful strike, which lasted from November 3 to November 7 and paralysed the traffic of a city with a population of 5,000,000 ... was carried through against the will of the social–fascist trade union bureaucracy." It continued: "Thanks to the correct application of united front tactics on the part of the R.T.U.O. in the period of the organisation of the strike, the National Socialist transport workers were drawn into the united proletarian front. There were even proletarian members of the National Socialist Party on the Central Strike Committee."[3]

Heinz Neumann was one of the leaders of the German Communist Party from 1928 to 1932. His widow, Margarete Buber Neumann, recalled years later that her husband told her in 1931 of a meeting in Moscow where Stalin had asked, "Don't you think that if National Socialism came to power in Germany, it would be so much taken up in the West that the Soviet Union could develop in peace and build up Socialism?"[4] We now have evidence from the Comintern archives that supports the idea that Stalin wanted Hitler to come to power in Germany. Heinz Neumann was removed by Stalin from the German Communist Party leadership in 1932. In exile in 1934, he wrote to the Comintern confessing that he was wrong in 1932 when he demanded that his fellow Communists "Hit the Fascists wherever you meet them."[5] Of course, how could you "hit the Fascists" when you join them on a strike committee against the Social Democrats?

Despite their support, when Hitler took over Germany, he wiped out the German Communists along with other opposition groups. In a speech on March 23, 1933, Hitler sent a clear message to Stalin, saying that Germany intended "maintaining friendly relations with foreign powers, without regard to the tendencies or general principles by which they are dominated, for *the elimination of Communism in Germany is a purely domestic German affair*" [italics in original].[6] Ernst Henry (whose real name was Semyon Rostovsky), a Soviet apparatchik in the Comintern who escaped from Germany after Hitler took power, explained in a 1988 interview that "the [German] Communists, clenching their teeth, fulfilled [Stalin's] order about the 'mortal combat' [against the Social Democrats]. An order is an order and party discipline is discipline. . . . [T]he theory of Social Fascism, month after month, was paving the road for Hitler. They [the Communists] clenched their fists, they subordinated themselves to [Stalin's] 'mind and will,' and went to face their death which was waiting for them in the SS prisons."[7]

Among the Western democracies, concern about the Soviet Union was forgotten as Hitler began invading neighboring countries. In 1935, the Soviet Union and the international Communist movement changed the Party line and organized an anti-Nazi united front with the Social Democrats, claiming to be the most active fighters against Nazism. The dishonesty of this claim became all too clear on August 23, 1939, when Stalin signed an alliance with Adolf Hitler. The world was shocked. Only the few who understood what had taken place in Germany a few years earlier were not surprised. And Stalin's goal of Soviet expansion was achieved: In a secret protocol to the pact, the German and Soviet dictatorships divided Poland between them and allowed the Soviet Union to conquer Estonia and Latvia. Lithuania was reserved for Nazi Germany, but in a subsequent agreement of September 28, 1939, the Nazis gave Lithuania to their Soviet ally in exchange for a larger share of Poland.[8] On June 19, 1940, *Moscow News* reported that the Red Army had entered Lithuania, Latvia, and Estonia to insure "mutual assistance pacts" between Russia and the Baltic States. Six days later the same news organ boasted: "Lithuanian, Latvian and Estonian Parliaments Proclaim Soviet Power, Ask to Join USSR."

Stalin ordered the Comintern to organize political support for the alliance with the Nazis. On September 7, 1939, George Dimitroff, General Secretary of the Comintern, met with Stalin, V. M. Molotov, and Andrei Zhdanov in the Kremlin. He recorded in his diary Stalin's explanation of the new Party line:

> The war is being conducted between two groups of capitalist states.... We have nothing against it when they mightily strike blows at each other and mutually weaken themselves. Not bad, if Germany would cause the position of the richest capitalist countries (particularly England) to totter. Hitler himself is shaking and undermining the capitalist system without understanding or wanting it.... The Communists of the capitalist countries must decisively come out against their own governments, against the war. Until the war, it was completely correct to juxtapose fascism with democratic regimes. During a war between the imperialist powers this is no longer correct. The differentiation of the capitalist countries into fascist and democratic has lost its previous meaning.... The Polish state was previously (in history) a national state. That is why revolutionaries defended it against division and enslavement. Today it is ... a fascist state that enslaves Ukrainians, White Russians, etc. The destruction of this state under the present conditions would mean one less bourgeois fascist state! What is bad if as a result of the smashing of Poland we expand the socialist system into new territories and populations?[9]

Stalin ordered that these themes be transmitted to the Communist parties as instructions.[10] On September 9, Dimitroff saw to this. The Communist parties of France and England were ordered to undermine the war efforts of their own countries and those in the United States.[11]

A secret radio message from Dimitroff to Earl Browder, head of the American Communist Party, read as follows: "The war created a new situation ... put aside the differences between the bourgeois-democratic states and the fascists. ... The tactic of the united front and democratic front is losing its significance. The question of fascism became a (sic) secondary significance."[12] On October 28, 1939, American Communists were instructed by Dimitroff that their slogan, "Keep the USA Out of the Imperialist War," should be interpreted widely to include opposition to U.S. arms being sent to the British and French.[13]

One radio message from Dimitroff to Browder instructed American Communists to defend the conquest of Poland by saying that it was a reactionary state, "built on the oppression of the Ukrainians, Belorussians (and) Jews," and that the Soviet Union saved eleven million people from the Polish State[14]—despite the fact that on December 5, 1939, the Soviets expelled one thousand Jews across the border to the Nazi side.[15] On Soviet instructions, the American Communists published Molotov's vile Supreme Soviet speech of October 31, 1939, where he said: "[O]ne swift blow to Poland, first by the German Army and then by the Red Army, and nothing was left of this ugly offspring of the Versailles Treaty. ... One may accept or reject the ideology of Hitlerism as well as any other ideological system; that is a matter of political views."[16] They also published Stalin's explanation of the Soviet position:

> It was not Germany that attacked France and England, but France and England that attacked Germany, thereby assuming responsibility for the present war; after hostilities had broken out, Germany made overtures of peace to France and England, and the Soviet Union openly supported Germany's peace overtures, for it considered, and continues to consider, that the earliest possible termination of the war would radically improve the position of all countries and nations; the ruling circles of England and France rudely rejected both Germany's peace overtures and the attempts of the Soviet Union to secure the earliest possible termination of the war. Such are the facts.[17]

Meanwhile, as ordered, the American Communist Party attacked President Roosevelt as a war monger for advocating American aid to the anti-Hitler Allies, and distributed pamphlets, leaflets, and pin-back buttons bearing the slogan, "The Yanks Are Not Coming!" By June 1940, the American Communists reported that they had distributed over three-and-one-half million anti-war pamphlets.[18] Eugene Dennis, an American Communist Party official, made a series of reports to the Presidium of the Executive Committee of the Comintern in April 1941. He described how his Party was carrying out its work: "The American Peace Mobilization, which was organized on the initiative of our Party in Chicago in September 1940, at a national anti-war conference . . . has become the main coordinating and leading center of the developing people's anti-imperialist and anti-war movement. The national leadership of the organization is of a broad, anti-imperialist, people's front character, in which the Communists and the left wing labor leaders play the leading role."[19] In another report, prepared for the same meeting, Dennis boasted of the position of the CIO "in defending the right to organize and strike in the war industries."[20] Communist trade union officials organized strikes to shut down defense plants.

British Communists not only attempted to undermine their country's war effort, but supplied Soviet military intelligence (GRU) with information that could be of use to Nazi Germany in its war against England. One spy ring, called "Group X," was headed by two British Communist Party officials, Professor J. B. S. Haldane (code name: *intelligentsia*), the chairman of the editorial board of the Party's paper, *The London Daily Worker,* and Ivor Montagu (code name: *nobility*), a writer who later became the President of the Party. Their work for Soviet intelligence was revealed by *Venona,* the secret messages sent between Moscow and their intelligence officers in the United States and England.[21] For instance, a GRU message to Moscow on September 10, 1940, conveyed a report on the extent of air raid damage to London docks and railroad stations. A week later, Montagu reported that the British had brought six destroyers into the Thames River.[22] On October 11, British Communists reported to the GRU that the aircraft factory in Rochester had been completely destroyed and that five thousand workers were being transferred to a new factory in Swindon,[23] thus providing the Nazis with their next target. And on October 16, Montagu reported that the British knew that German bombers were being guided by a radio beam—a fact the British considered highly classified as they worked to develop countermeasures.[24]

On June 22, 1941, Nazi Germany attacked the Soviet Union. During the post-Cold War period of "glasnost," Russian historians provided evidence from their archives that explained the disastrous losses, including millions of POWs, the Soviets suffered in the early days of the war. Writing in the *Soviet Military History Journal* in June 1988, Lieutenant General M. M. Kiryan revealed that

> As a result of the enemy surprise attack, the border district troops were unable to bring themselves to combat readiness, to deploy and take up the defensive lines. . . . The combat equipment was in parking areas, as a rule, in mothballs. The divisions and regiments had one unit of fire of ammunition and one tank of fuel. The remaining supplies were stored as the army and district and corps as well as the anti-aircraft artillery, including the national air defense artillery, were concentrated in camps at planned training assemblies a significant distance away from their units and formations. For this reason the troops entered combat without proper artillery support and, as a rule, without an anti-aircraft artillery cover.[25]

During the purges of the late 1930s, Stalin had ordered over forty thousand Soviet military and intelligence officers executed.[26] Despite these heavy losses, important Soviet spies still functioned, and they had provided Stalin with ample warning of the attack. He chose not to believe them, however, trusting instead his fellow dictator Adolf

Hitler. On June 11, Soviet intelligence reported that their source at German Air Force headquarters (Harro Schulze-Boysen) had warned of the possibility of a surprise attack. Stalin wrote on one of the reports, "you can tell your 'source' at German Air Force headquarters to go [obscenity deleted] himself. He is no 'source,' he is spreading disinformation."[27] Two days before the invasion, Richard Sorge, the Soviet Union's most important spy in Japan, reported from Tokyo that the German ambassador had told him that Germany was ready to attack the Soviet Union.[28] Both Schulze-Boysen and Sorge were risking their lives to provide Stalin with information that he didn't believe. Both were later captured and killed while continuing to spy for Stalin.

On the day of the Nazi attack, Stalin ordered Dimitroff to instruct the Communist parties to change their line again and to devote their full energy in support of the anti-Nazi war.[29] Thus a directive to the British Communists read as follows:

> The sudden attack of Germany on the Soviet Union is not only a blow against the socialist country, but also against the freedom and independence of all peoples. . . . It is necessary to do everything to support the Soviet people in its just war, and also to oppose all anti-Soviet plans and actions in your country. It is necessary to spread a mass movement under the slogan of the creation of a united international front of people's struggle against the German fascists to protect all the peoples oppressed by fascism and support the Soviet people. Take into account that at the present moment the question is the protection of the peoples from the fascist enslavement, and not the socialist revolution.[30]

As a result of such directives, the American Peace Mobilization, with the same officers and the same address, changed its name to the "American People's Mobilization for Victory over Fascism."

Richard Sorge reported to Moscow, in early 1941, that the Japanese had decided to make war on the U.S. rather than attack the

Soviet Union. He warned, however, that this decision was reversible. Two experienced intelligence officers in Moscow, Iskhak Akhmerov and Vassiliy Zarubin, had served in the U.S. and set to thinking of ways to keep the Japanese focused against America. Akhmerov had worked with a Soviet spy named Harry Dexter White, a high official of the U.S. Treasury Department. With the permission of Lavrenti Beria, Stalin's chief of espionage and internal repression, a young intelligence officer, Vitaliy Pavlov, was dispatched to Washington to use White to promote ideas that would exacerbate Japanese–American tensions. White used these ideas in a memo to his boss and close friend, Secretary of Treasury Henry Morgenthau. They included a demand that Japan withdraw its military from China, Indo–China, and Thailand, lease to the U.S. up to 50 percent of Japanese naval vessels and airplanes, and sell to the U.S. half of Japan's output of war material.[31] Morgenthau did not use the memo at that time. But when Germany attacked the Soviet Union, it became even more important to Moscow that Japan concentrate on the U.S. White rewrote the memo and Morgenthau passed it to President Roosevelt, who in turn gave it to Secretary of State Cordell Hull. Using much of the harsh language, Hull wrote an ultimatum to the Japanese on November 26, 1941,[32] which ultimatum was used by the Japanese "war party" to override those in Tokyo who objected to the plan to attack Pearl Harbor.

In Nazi-occupied Europe, Communists were ordered to organize guerrilla warfare to hold down Nazi troops.[33] In Yugoslavia, the Communists were a tiny group. Their leaders, including General Secretary Milan Gorkic, previously had been executed in Moscow on Stalin's orders.[34] Josip Broz, later known as Tito, was appointed by Moscow to head the Party and sent back to Yugoslavia in 1938.[35] On March 29, 1941, Dimitroff ordered Tito and the Yugoslav Communists to avoid public Communist activities, even street demonstrations, and to remain quiet.[36] With the Nazi attack on the Soviet Union, new orders were issued. Tito explained in 1948:

On June 22, 1941, Hitler's fascist hordes carried out a sneak attack on the Soviet Union. The Politbureau had a session the same day and the new situation, as well as the measures our Party had to take in this connection, were discussed. It was determined that the CCCPY (Central Committee of the Communist Party of Yugoslavia) and other central and provincial committees would publish proclamations calling the people to armed struggle, to a general people's uprising.[37]

Stalin had used his alliance with Hitler to conquer new territory for the Soviet Union, and he saw the opportunity to use his alliance against Hitler for the same end. Yugoslavia was an important target. A worldwide propaganda campaign was conducted to portray Tito as an important anti-Nazi hero. In the U.S., for instance, Communist Party member Howard Fast wrote a book titled *The Incredible Tito, Man of the Hour*.[38] In 1944, Manya Reiss, using the name Maria Aerova, was an American Communist Party representative to Institute 205 in Moscow, the secret apparatus that had replaced the supposedly abolished Comintern. On August 24, she wrote a memo to the leadership about Fast's book: "*The Incredible Tito* is a brief story of the national liberation war of the Yugoslavian people. Tito is depicted as the implementation of the aspiration of the people of Yugoslavia for national independence and democratic freedom."[39] But as late as March 1945, Tito, remembering the fate of his predecessors, radioed to Moscow, "In what relationship do I stand to Filippov?"[40] Filippov was the code name for Stalin. And indeed, Tito had reason to worry, for Stalin managed the Communist Party in Yugoslavia as he did every Communist Party. Only he could decide Tito's role.

Yugoslavia's King Peter was in England, and the British were providing support to the Chetniks—the underground led by Draza Mihailovich, who fought the Nazis long before the Communists began their uprising. The Communists, called the Partisans, needed British support to allow them to take over postwar Yugoslavia. Tito, guided by Moscow, worked to get the British to transfer their support to him. In December 1943, Yugoslav government officials, working with the British in Cairo, asked the Yugoslav Communists a series of questions, including whether they were going to carry out propaganda against the king. Tito advised Moscow that he had answered that the question of the monarchy should be settled after the war, based on whether the king had helped or opposed the "forces of the people both in the country and abroad."[41] Moscow answered: "Your answers to the three Cairo questions are correct. It is desirable, however, to show a necessary flexibility with reference to the question of propaganda against the King, in order better to disorganize his supporters abroad and in Serbia, and more easily to overcome certain difficulties on the side of the British and Americans in the matter of their material assistance to [Tito's movement]."[42]

By February 1944, Stalin knew that the British were prepared to abandon the Chetniks and support Tito's Partisans. Dimitroff, on Stalin's orders, instructed Tito to take a harder line against the king and the non-Communist forces fighting the Nazis. Dimitroff radioed:

> We have received your enquiry regarding the attitude to be adopted towards King Peter. I am communicating our common opinion, including the opinion of the comrade you named, whom we ask you in future to name in your messages as DRUG [*Friend*—the new code name for Stalin].
>
> 1. AVNOJ (Anti-Fascist Council of National Liberation) of Yugoslavia [Tito's forces], in just the same way as the Englishman who is well known to you [Churchill], stands for the unity of Yugoslavs; but while there are two governments, one in Yugoslavia and the other in Cairo, there can be no unity. Therefore the government in Cairo must be set aside, including also D. Mihailovich. . . .
>
> 2. The government in Yugoslavia, that is to say AVNOJ of Yugoslavia, must be recognised by the English and other allies as the sole government of Yugoslavia, in which case the King must submit to the laws of AVNOJ of Yugoslavia.

3. If King Peter accepts all these conditions, then AVNOJ of Yugoslavia has nothing against collaborating with him on condition that the question of the monarchy in Yugoslavia is settled by the people after the liberation of Yugoslavia. Such is our view. Please acknowledge receipt urgently.[43]

A few days later, Tito radioed Moscow with the text of a message sent him by Churchill. The British Prime Minister said that he was sending his son, Major Randolph Churchill, and other officers to serve on Tito's staff, and that the British would support Tito's faction. Regarding the king, he said, "It would not be chivalrous for Great Britain to throw him on one side. We cannot demand that he break all his existing connections with his country. I hope that you will understand that."[44] On April 26, Tito wrote to Dimitroff that Randolph Churchill had made several visits to Partisan units. "[T]hese visits," he said, "as well as being a mark of recognition on the part of our allies, were also a proof of hardy cooperation between our movement and our great allies."[45]

David Martin, an American expert on Yugoslavia, concluded that the British decision to abandon the non-Communist Yugoslavs was in part influenced by Soviet agents in Great Britain. In the last of three books he wrote between 1946 and 1990, Martin identified James Klugmann as one of the Soviet agents in British intelligence in Cairo who had helped distort Churchill's view of the Yugoslav situation.[46] After World War II, Klugmann became a member of the Executive Committee of the British Communist Party.[47] Martin also argues, with substantial evidence, that it was the Chetniks rather than the Partisans who carried out the war against the Nazi occupiers. As for the liberation of Belgrade, the story is told by Soviet General Shtemenko: Tito's forces had joined with the invading Soviet Army, but were soon left behind as they "had neither tanks nor motor vehicles, (and) could not keep up with the Soviet tanks." When this was reported to Moscow, Soviet General Korneyev was ordered "to mount the Yugoslav infantry on our tanks and jointly to take Belgrade with utmost speed."[48] Tito's later claim that his partisan forces had defeated the Germans in Yugoslavia and liberated Belgrade was simply not true. Stalin's Red Army put Tito in power.

Tito was Stalin's creature. But after the war, he began to believe his own propaganda. His righthand man, Edvard Kardelj, speaking at a Communist Party Central Committee meeting on April 12, 1948, claimed that "Yugoslavia was the country that freed almost the whole of her territory during the war with her own forces. Czechoslovakia, Rumania, Bulgaria, Poland, Hungary were freed by the Red Army."[49] Stalin responded on May 4, in a letter to the Yugoslav Communist Party:

> . . . the fact that after the Headquarters of the Yugoslav partisans had been routed by the German paratroops, at a moment when the national liberation movement of Yugoslavia was experiencing a serious crisis, the Soviet Army came to the help of the Yugoslav people, routed the German occupier, liberated Belgrade and thus created the conditions indispensable to the Communist Party for taking power. Unfortunately the Soviet Army did not and could not offer such help to the French and Italian Communist parties. If Comrades Tito and Kardelj were to take this circumstance into consideration as an indisputable fact, they would clamour less about their merits and would comport themselves more befittingly and modestly.[50]

As in all Communist dictatorships, Tito, on taking power, conducted a campaign to wipe out those who might oppose him. The first target was Draza Mihailovich, who organized the Chetnicks. Mihailovich was captured by the Communists and placed on trial in a Moscow-style court. Unlike some others, he refused to plead guilty and gave answers to questions that annoyed his jailers. When asked when his Chetnik fighters made first contact with Tito's Partisans, he answered that it was "after the Soviet Union had entered the war.

It might have been sometime after June 22, 1941." He was reminding them that while he and his forces fought the Nazis from the beginning, the Communist Partisans only became involved when the Soviet Union was in danger. He was convicted and shot.[51]

The Catholic Church also became a target. The arrest and trial of Archbishop Aloysius Stepinac, a Croat nationalist, shocked the U.S. The Yugoslav government published a booklet accusing Stepinac of being complicit in the atrocities committed against Jews and Serbs by the pro-Nazi government of Croatia.[52] Years later, the Yugoslav Communists inadvertently provided the evidence that these charges were false: Andrija Artukovic, Minister of the Interior of the puppet Croatian government during Nazi occupation, escaped to the U.S. In the late 1950s, the Yugoslav government wanted him extradited to face trial, and in the material they supplied against Artukovic was a letter to him from Stepinac, protesting what was happening to Serbs and Jews in the concentration camp of Jasenvac. "Jasenvac camp," he wrote, "is a shameful stain on the honor of the Independent State of Croatia. It is a disgrace to Croatia." In another letter he wrote, "already there are so many measures that those who know the situation will say that not even in Germany were the racial laws applied with such rigor and speed. I do not think it can bring us any glory if it is said of us that we have solved the Jewish problem in the most radical way, that is to say, the cruelest."[53]

Stalin lost control of Yugoslavia in 1948, as Tito took his country out of the Soviet bloc. But Stalin retained control of the rest of the Central European countries "liberated" by the Red Army. Most important was Poland. In 1944, the Russians claimed that "The Soviet government . . . does not pursue the aim of acquiring any part of Polish territory whatever, or of altering the social system in Poland. . . ."[54] But in fact, from the beginning of the war, the Soviets arrested and, in some cases, executed Poles who might challenge their future rule. Among those arrested in 1940 was the young Polish Zionist Menachen Begin, later Prime Minister of Israel. His moving book, *White Nights, The Story of a Prisoner in Russia,* gives us an interesting insight into Soviet thinking and brutality.[55] Most of the Polish Jews arrested by the Soviet secret police were not Zionists, but leaders of other political groups, who, like their Christian fellow victims, were viewed as threats to Soviet power. Henryk Erlich and Victor Alter, leaders of the General Jewish Workers Union of Poland, the Bund, were arrested by the Soviet secret police in June 1941 and sentenced to death. A few weeks later, their sentences were commuted to ten years of hard labor in the gulag. After the Nazi attack on the Soviet Union, they were released and ordered by the Russians to organize a Jewish Anti-Fascist Committee to urge Jews in the West to support the Soviet war effort. In December 1941, they were again arrested, and leadership of the Jewish Anti-Fascist Committee was taken over by dedicated Soviet Communists.

Erlich and Alter were well known to Jewish and trade union leaders in the West. When they disappeared, trade union officials such as William Green of the AFL, Philip Murray of the CIO, and David Dubinsky of the International Ladies' Garment Workers' Union appealed to the Soviet government for their release. They were not answered until February 1943, when Maxim Litvinov wrote to Green that the two men had been executed due to "their hostile activities, including appeals to the Soviet troops to stop bloodshed and immediately to conclude peace with Germany."[56] This was, of course, nonsense. Their only appeals were to Western Jews and trade unionists to support the Soviet war effort. There was a tremendous outcry against the executions in the American and British trade union communities. The American Communists responded with a statement of "Jewish Unionists on Alter–Erlich," signed by one hundred union officials, most of them members of the Communist Party.[57] The Polish government–in–exile protested the executions in a note of March 8, 1943, to the Soviet government:

> The political and social activities of Messrs. Alter and Ehr-
> lich for many years were well-known throughout Poland and
> in international labor circles. Their patriotism and loyalty as

Polish citizens during the German invasion of Poland, and also in the light of the desolation caused throughout the Polish nation and the Jewish population by that invasion, are absolute guarantees that they could not even indirectly have been sympathizers with or tools of any action whatsoever in favor of Germany, and even less so in favor of Hitlerism. . . .

On the contrary, it was well-known to the government of the Union of Soviet Socialist Republics that during the period between their release from prison and their re-arrest in December 1941, Henryk Ehrlich and Victor Alter proceeded, with the knowledge and consent of the Soviet authorities, to organize in Moscow an International Jewish Anti-Fascist Committee, the object of which was to unite all Jewish masses throughout the world in the war effort against Germany and Hitlerism.[58]

The Soviet government, in a note dated March 31, rejected the protest and insisted that the two Jewish socialists were conspiring to aid the Nazis.[59]

In April 1943, the Nazis announced that they had found mass graves of Polish Army officers in Katyn Forest, near the Soviet city of Smolensk. As part of the Soviet program of liquidating potential opponents in the territory they controlled, about fifteen thousand Polish officers, many of them intellectuals, were murdered by the Soviet secret police. The Nazis, who had murdered so many millions themselves, saw the opportunity for propaganda against the Soviet Union. They brought foreign doctors, and even American and British POWs who were medical officers, to observe the exhumation of the bodies.[60] The Polish government–in–exile suggested that the International Red Cross be brought in to determine who was to blame. The Soviets accused the Nazis of the atrocity and took the opportunity to break relations with the Polish government–in–exile for even asking for an investigation.[61]

The pro-Soviet Corliss Lamont, in a pamphlet for *Soviet Russia Today*, quoted the *New York Herald Tribune* as calling it "a safe assumption that the Poles would not have taken so tough an attitude toward the Soviet Government if it had not been for the widespread support Americans have been giving them in the cases of Henry Ehrlich and Victor Alter."[62] We now know that the foreign editor of the *New York Herald Tribune*, Joseph Barnes, was identified by Whittaker Chambers as a member of a Communist Party underground group working for Soviet Military Intelligence.[63] Other Americans also assisted the Soviet propaganda effort to deny responsibility for the Katyn Forest massacre. Alan Cranston, then the head of the Foreign Language Division of the Office of War Information and later United States Senator from California, tried to pressure Polish language radio stations in the U.S. to refrain from blaming the Russians. Joseph Lang, the General Manager of New York radio station WHOM and a volunteer official of the Foreign Language Radio Wartime Control, testified that Cranston met with him and demanded that he "straighten out the situation in Detroit," where "Polish news commentators had taken a rather antagonistic attitude toward Russia in this matter...." Cranston said that this "was inimical to the war effort and should be straightened out in some way." According to Lang, Cranston wanted a gag put on the Polish broadcasters who accused the Soviet Union of the crime.[64]

In 1944, the Soviets had retaken the Smolensk area and conducted their own investigation of the killings of the Polish officers. They concluded, of course, that the Nazis were responsible.[65] U.S. Ambassador to the Soviet Union Averell Harriman sent his young daughter Kathleen to represent the U.S. embassy at this investigation. She concluded that the Nazis were guilty because the bodies were laid out in a "methodical manner." In 1952, she testified before Congress that having examined the evidence years later, her opinion was "that the Russians did kill the Poles." When asked by a congressman why her father had sent her instead of "somebody older and somebody who, perhaps, was a medical authority," she answered:

"My impression is that he selected me because he thought it would be more difficult for them to refuse him if he asked that I go than if he asked a medical officer or somebody else."[66] The Congressional Committee, after extensive investigation, concluded that the Soviets committed the murders. During the period of glasnost, the Soviets confessed that the murders were committed by the Soviet NKVD (People's Commissariat of Internal Affairs). Documents concerning the atrocity were published by researcher Nataliya Lebedeva in the official Soviet magazine *International Affairs* in June 1990.[67] Documents were also found showing that Stalin personally ordered the killings. Once again, the NKVD wiped out people who had the intellect and ability to oppose Soviet rule in their countries.

The Nazis derived so much valuable propaganda from the revelation of the Katyn massacre that they decided to reveal a similar case in the Ukraine. They had discovered mass graves with eleven to twelve thousand corpses near the Ukrainian town of Vinnytsia. This was in Eastern Ukraine—part of the prewar Soviet Union—and the victims had been killed between 1936 and 1938.[68] Apollon Trembow, who used the *non de plume* Petro Pavlovych, testified in 1959 before the House Committee on Un-American Activities about his experience in the Ukraine in 1938. He said that he and others did not understand at that time "why so many were arrested, especially Ukrainians, those of Polish descent—half Polish, half Ukrainian and many Jewish people who were arrested in our town as well as other towns within the Vinnitsa Province."[69] One witness who provided information years later to the Ukrainian Historical Association asked to remain anonymous. He had been a correspondent of the Ukrainian newspaper *Vinnytski Visty*, and had access to the lists that the Nazis compiled of the victims. He described being called to the office of the local Nazi officials and instructed to report the nationality of Polish and Ukrainian victims, but to list Russians, Jews, and Gypsies as "nationality unknown."[70] The truth—that the Communists murdered Jews—contradicted Nazi propaganda.

The Polish Home Army had fought underground against the Nazis since 1939, supported by the Polish government–in–exile. After the Nazi attack on the Soviet Union, the Comintern air-dropped agents to organize Communist Partisan groups. By 1944, a number of such units were operating and the Red Army was pushing the Germans back. In February 1944, the Polish Communists radioed Moscow that the regional commander of the Home Army had contacted them to coordinate the anti-Nazi fight. They suggested that if several thousand weapons could be dropped to them, they could organize cooperation with the Home Army, which they referred to as "hostile military organizations." But they said that they would carry out "the liquidation of the 'elite' and the most intractable elements. . . ."[71]

In August 1944, with the Nazis weakened by a war on two fronts and the Red Army fighting on Polish territory, the Polish Home Army began a revolt against Nazi forces in Warsaw. Stalin halted the Red Army in order to give the Nazis time to wipe out the non-Communist Polish fighters. Roosevelt and Churchill wrote to Stalin on August 20, 1944, "We are thinking of world opinion if anti-Nazis in Warsaw are in effect abandoned. We believe that all three of us should do the utmost to save as many of the patriots there as possible. We hope that you will drop immediate supplies and munitions to the patriot Poles of Warsaw, or will you agree to help our planes in doing it very quickly? We hope you will approve. The time element is of extreme importance."[72] Stalin's response was an insulting refusal. He wrote, "Sooner or later the truth about the handful of power-seeking criminals who launched the Warsaw adventure will out. Those elements, playing on the credulity of the inhabitants of Warsaw, exposed practically unarmed people to German guns, armour and aircraft." He claimed that the uprising benefited not the Poles but "the Hitlerites."[73]

The Poles kept asking for arms and supplies, and the British government pressed the U.S. to help. Some American military officials, concerned about the danger to their planes, also opposed air drops. On September 11, General F. L. Anderson, an official of the

U.S. Strategic Air Force in Europe, met with Harry Hopkins, President Roosevelt's closest friend and advisor. The General expressed opposition to the air drops and Hopkins agreed. More significantly, according to Anderson, Hopkins said "that he would see that any cablegrams, whether they came from Mr. Churchill or from [U.S. Ambassador] Mr. Winant, would be held in abeyance and that we would not be committed to do this job."[74] Hopkins had enormous influence on President Roosevelt and apparently felt that he could conceal even Churchill's requests from the president.

In May 1945, President Truman sent Hopkins to Moscow to meet with Stalin. According to the notes of Assistant Secretary of State Charles Bohlen, despite the U.S. position that there should be free elections in Poland, Hopkins told Stalin "that the United States would desire a Poland friendly to the Soviet Union and in fact desire to see friendly countries all along the Soviet borders." Stalin replied: "If that be so we can easily come to terms in regard to Poland."[75] Free elections were not held in Poland and Stalin established a Communist dictatorship there. Such incidents convinced some scholars that Hopkins was a Russophile, or perhaps worse.[76] Evidence now available shows that he was a Soviet agent. An intercepted Soviet intelligence communication of May 29, 1943, revealed that a Soviet spy called "Agent 19" had reported to Iskhak Akhmerov that he had attended a meeting with Roosevelt and Churchill, where the plans for D-Day were discussed. That was the most sensitive military secret at that time. Examination of the records of the Roosevelt–Churchill meetings reveal that the third man was Harry Hopkins.[77] This confirmed a statement that Akhmerov later made to a KGB training class, that Hopkins was "the most important of all Soviet wartime agents in the United States." Oleg Gordievsky, a courageous KGB officer who spied against the Soviets for British Intelligence for over ten years, was a student in that class and reported Akhmerov's revelation to British and American officials.[78] There is no innocent explanation for Hopkins supplying classified information to Akhmerov, or even meeting with the Soviet intelligence officer. Akhmerov was under deep cover and concealed his identity from the U.S. government.

On July 31, 1944, Soviet agent Harry Dexter White met with a Soviet intelligence officer, code named "Koltsov." He explained that he and Treasury Secretary Morgenthau were leaving for London and Normandy on August 5. This was reported by cable to Moscow.[79] On August 7, White and Morgenthau met with General Dwight Eisenhower, who revealed that he was opposed to a soft peace for Germany. Based on this discussion, White developed the so-called Morgenthau Plan to strip German industry and make it an agricultural country. The plan was to convert Germany into a pasture and reduce it to a fifth-rate power.[80] After careful study, Roosevelt and Churchill rejected this still-secret plan. But a leak to the press from the Treasury Department on September 23, 1944, suggested that the rejected plan was in fact U.S. government policy. The Nazi propaganda machine turned the story into a plot by the "Jew" Morgenthau to destroy Germany. This helped strengthen German resistance to the Allied armies and cost British and American lives. U.S. propaganda responded with President Roosevelt's announcement that the Allies "had absolutely no intention of enslaving the German people."[81] Nevertheless, lives were lost because of the subversive activities of Harry Dexter White.

In 1943, Stalin decided that the Comintern would be terminated. In reality, control of the foreign Communist parties would be secretly carried out by the new Institute 205, which, like the Comintern, would be headed by George Dimitroff, with the help of high-level Soviet officials. Stalin's idea to replace the Comintern was hatched originally in 1941, based on the argument that much anti-Communist propaganda would be refuted if there appeared to be no Communist International to direct foreign parties.[82] Two years later, after the termination was announced, Dimitroff met with Pavel Fitin, the head of the Foreign Department of the NKVD, to continue the use of secret intelligence channels to transmit orders to the parties. The next day he met with Lieutenant General Ivan Iylitshov and Colonel Ivan

Bolshakov, the head and deputy head of Soviet Military Intelligence, to insure their continued assistance to the secret Institute 205.[83] After World War II, Stalin sent Dimitroff back to Bulgaria to act as the Communist dictator of that country. In September 1947, under the leadership of Andri Zhdanov, a meeting was held in Poland to establish the Communist Information Bureau (Cominform). It consisted of the ruling Communist parties of East and Central Europe and of Italy and France.[84] In 1949, the official Cominform newspaper, *For Lasting Peace for a People's Democracy*, reported that Maurice Thorez and Palmiro Togliatti, General Secretaries of the French and Italian Communist parties, respectively, had announced that if the Soviet Red Army entered their countries in the course of a war against the West, the working people would welcome them.[85]

The Cold War is customarily considered the post-World War II period of confrontation between the Soviet Union and the Western democracies. In a larger sense, however, the Cold War started in 1919, when the Comintern was organized in Moscow, continued without pause through the 1930s and through World War II, and lasted until the Soviet Union collapsed on August 21, 1991.

Notes

The **Communist International Archives** are found in the Russian Center for the Preservation and Study of Documents of Recent History in Moscow. Some of the most interesting sections which we used in 1992 and 1993 have now been closed.

Venona was the name used by the America code breakers for the decrypted communications between the NKVD in Moscow and their officers in the United States during World War II.

ISCOT was the name used by the British code breakers for decrypted communications between Moscow and the Communist underground groups in Europe during World War II.

Venona and ISCOT may be found at the National Security Agency Library and Museum at Fort Meade, Maryland.

1. J. V. Stalin, *Works*, Vol. 10 (Moscow: Foreign Languages Publishing House, 1954), pp. 293–49.

2. S. Gusev, *The Next Step In Britain, America and Ireland, Speeches and Reports, Twelfth Plenum of the E.C.C.I.* (New York: Workers Library Publishers, 1932), p. 9.

3. *R.I.L.U. Magazine* (London), January 1, 1933: 952, 957. (The magazine was edited in Moscow and the English language edition published in London.)

4. Margarete Buber, *Under Two Dictators* (London: Victor Gollance Ltd., 1950), p. xi.

5. Communist International Archives, Moscow, Fond 495, Opus 19, Delo 706, p. 10.

6. *The New Germany Desires Work and Peace, Speeches by Reich Chancellor Adolf Hitler the Leader of the New Germany* (Berlin: Liebheit & Thiesen, 1934), p. 17.

7. *Literaturnyi Kirgizstan* (in Russian) Frunze, USSR, March 1988.

8. Nazi–Soviet Relations, 1939–1941, Documents from the Archives of The German Foreign Office, United States Department of State, Washington D.C., 1948, pp 78 and 107.

9. Georgi Dimitroff, *Tagebücher* 1933–1943 (Berlin: Aufbau-Verlag, 2000), pp. 273–74.

10. Ibid.

11. Communist International Archives, Moscow, Fond 495, Opus 18, Delo 1291.

12. Communist International Archives, Moscow, Fond 495, Opus 184, Delo 8.

13. Communist International Archives, Moscow, Fond 495, Opus 20, Delo 538.

14. Communist International Archives, Moscow, Fond 495, Opus 74, Delo 469.

15. *Moscow News*, June 2–9, 1991.

16. V. M. Molotov, *Molotov's Report to the Supreme Soviet* (New York: Workers Library Publishers, 1939), pp. 4, 6.

17. M. Ross, *A History of Soviet Foreign Policy* (New York: Workers Library Publishers, 1940), pp. 44–45.

18. *Daily Worker* (New York), June 1, 1940.

19. T. Ryan (Eugene Dennis) "The Political Situation in the U.S.A. and the Work and Tasks of the CP USA—Draft Report for the Presidium," April 7, 1941, p. 27. Communist International Archives, Moscow, Fond 515, Opus 1, Delo 4091. Marked Confidential.

20. T. Ryan (Eugene Dennis) "The Situation Within the CIO," March 29, 1941, pp. 1–2. Communist International Archives, Moscow, Fond 515, Opus 1, Delo 4091. Marked Confidential.

21. The *Venona* messages were decrypted by American and British code breakers and released in 1995. See Herbert Romerstein and Eric Breindel, *The Venona Secrets, Exposing Soviet Espionage and America's Traitors* (Washington, D.C.: Regnery Publishing Co., 2000).

22. *Venona*, London to Moscow, September 17, 1940.

23. *Venona*, London to Moscow, October 11, 1940.

24. *Venona*, London to Moscow, October 16, 1940.

25. *Voyenno-Istoricheskiy Zhurnal* (Moscow), June 1988.

26. *Krasnaya Zvezda*, Moscow, June 22, 1988.

27. *Izvestiya Tsk KPSS*, Moscow, April 1990.

28. Ibid.

29. Dimitroff, *Tagebücher*, pp. 392–93.

30. Memorandum from Dimitroff to Stalin, June 25, 1941. Communist International Archives, Moscow, Fond 495, Opus 73, Delo 112, pp. 1–2.

31. Vitaliy Pavlov, *Operatziya "Sneg,"* Geya, Moscow, 1996, p. 39; and Harry Dexter White memo to Secretary Henry Morgenthau, Jr., May 1941, *Morgenthau Diaries* (manuscript), Vol. 405, pp. 471ff, Roosevelt Library, Hyde Park, New York.

32. *Pearl Harbor Attack Hearings Before the Joint Committee on the Investigation of the Pearl Harbor Attack,* Washington D.C., 1946, Part 19, pp. 3652ff & 3667ff.

33. Dimitroff, *Tagebücher,* p. 399.

34. Branko Lazitch and Milorad M. Drachkovitch, *Biographical Dictionary of the Comintern* (Stanford, CA: Hoover Institution Press, 1986), p. 148; and Pero Simic, "An Unknown Tito," *New Times* (Moscow), October 16–22, 1990: 36.

35. Ibid., Simic, p. 37.

36. Dimitroff, *Tagebücher,* p. 365.

37. Josip Broz Tito, *Political Report of the Central Committee of the Communist Party of Yugoslavia, Report delivered at the V Congress of the CPY,* Beograd, 1948, p. 51.

38. Howard Fast, *The Incredible Tito: Man of the Hour* (New York: Magazine House, 1944).

39. Communist International Archives, Moscow, Fond 495, Opus 74, Delo 487.

40. ISCOT No. 1323, Yugoslavia to Moscow, March 11, 1945. (ISCOT was the name for the coded radio messages sent between Moscow and the Communist parties in Nazi-occupied Europe and decrypted by British Intelligence.)

41. ISCOT No. 304, Yugoslavia to Moscow, December 24, 1943.

42. ISCOT No. 1459, Moscow to Tito, December 28, 1943.

43. ISCOT No. 1300, Dimitroff to Tito, February 9, 1944.

44. ISCOT No. 308, Yugoslavia to Moscow, February 14, 1944.

45. ISCOT No. 109, Yugoslavia to Moscow, April 26, 1944.

46. David Martin, *Ally Betrayed, The Uncensored Story of Tito and Mihailovich* (New York: Prentice-Hall, Inc., 1946); David Martin, *Patriot or Traitor, The Case of General Mihailovich* (Stanford, CA: Hoover Institution Press, 1979); and David Martin, *The Web of Disinformation, Churchill's Yugoslav Blunder* (San Diego, New York, London: Harcourt Brace Jovanovich, Publishers, 1990).

47. For example, see *Twenty-sixth Congress of the Communist Party,* March 27–30, 1959, London.

48. Ibid., p. 24.

49. Vladimir Dedijer, *Tito* (New York: Simon & Schuster, 1953), p. 339.

50. Letters of the CC CPY and the CC CPSU(b), Beograd, 1948, p. 87.

51. *The Trial of Dragoljub-Draza Mihailovic,* Stenographic Record and Documents, Belgrade, 1946, pp. 110, 5439.

52. *The Case of Archbishop Stepinac,* Embassy of the Federal Peoples Republic of Yugoslavia, Washington, D.C., 1947, p. 50.

53. *Yugoslav Facts & Views,* "Who is Andrija Artukovic," February 18, 1958, distributed by the Yugoslav Embassy, Washington, DC.

54. "Soviet-Polish Relations, A Collection of Official Documents 1944–1946," *Soviet News* (official London Soviet Embassy publication), London, 1946, p. 4.

55. Menachem Begin, *White Nights, The Story of a Prisoner in Russia* (New York: Harper & Row, Publishers, 1979).

56. *The Case of Henryk Erlich and Victor Alter* (New York: The American Representation of General Jewish Workers Union of Poland, 1943).

57. *Daily Worker*, March 25, 1943: 2.

58. *Polish–Soviet Relations 1918–1943*, Official Documents, Polish Embassy, Washington, circa 1943, pp. 178–80. (The varied spelling of the names is a result of transliteration from different European languages.)

59. Ibid.

60. *Amtliches Material zum Massenmord von Katyn* (Berlin: Gedruckt im Deutschen Verlag, 1943).

61. See *Polish–Soviet Relations, 1918–1943*, pp. 245–46.

62. Alter Brody, *Behind the Polish–Soviet Break*, Introduction by Corliss Lamont, (New York: Soviet Russia Today, 1943), p. 2.

63. Whittaker Chambers, Comprehensive Statement to FBI, January 3 to April 18, 1949, p. 148.

64. House of Representatives Select Committee to Investigate the Federal Communications Commission, *Study and Investigation of the National Communications Commission*, August 5, 1943, Testimony of Joseph Lang, pp. 387–89.

65. "The Truth About Katyn, Report of Special Commission for Ascertaining and Investigating the Circumstances of the Shooting of Polish Officer Prisoners by the German–Fascist Invaders in the Katyn Forest," *Soviet War News* (issued by Soviet Embassy), London, 1944.

66. *The Katyn Forest Massacre, Hearings before the Select Committee to Conduct an Investigation of the Facts, Evidence, and Circumstances of the Katyn Forest Massacre*, June and November 1952, Part 7, pp. 2143 & 2147.

67. Nataliya Lebedeva, "The Katyn Tragedy," *International Affairs* (Moscow), June 1990: 98ff.

68. *Amtliches Material zum Massenmord von Winniza*, Berlin, 1944,

69. *The Crimes of Khrushchev*, Part 2, Committee on Un-American Activities House of Representatives, September 1959, p. 18.

70. Ihor Kamensetsky, *The Tragedy of Vinnytsia, Materials on Stalin's Policy of Extermination in Ukraine During the Great Purge, 1936–1938* (Toronto, New York: Ukrainian Historical Association, 1989), p. 61.

71. ISCOT Numbers 851 and 838, Poland to Moscow, February 23, 1944.

72. *Correspondence Between the Chairman of the Council of Ministers of the U.S.S.R. and the Presidents of the U.S.A. and the Prime Ministers of Great Britain During the Great Patriotic War of 1941–1945*, Vol. II (Moscow: Foreign Languages Publishing House, 1957), p. 156.

73. Ibid., p. 157.

74. Memo of General F. L. Anderson on his meeting with Harry Hopkins, September 7, 1944, in Carl Spaatz papers, Library of Congress, Box 182.

75. *Foreign Relations of the United States, Diplomatic Papers, The Conference of Berlin [Potsdam Conference], 1945* (Washington, D.C.: Government Printing Office, 1960), vol. 1, p. 28.

76. See, for example, George N. Crocker, *Roosevelt's Road to Russia* (Chicago: Henry Regnery Company, 1959).

77. *Venona*, New York to Moscow, May 29, 1943.

78. Christopher Andrew and Oleg Gordievsky, *KGB, The Inside Story* (New York: HarperCollins, 1990), pp. 287–88.

79. *Venona*, New York to Moscow, August 4–5, 1944, and New York to Moscow October 1, 1944.

80. Senate Internal Security Sub-Committee, Interlocking Subversion in Government Departments, Part 30, pp. 2639–40. Reprint of article from *United Nations World*.

81. *Frontpost Nachrichten fur Deutsche Soldaten. Herausgeber: Die Amerikanischen Truppen in Westeuropa*, October 25, 1944.

82. Dimitroff, *Tagebücher*, pp. 386–87.

83. Ibid., pp. 707–8.

84. A. Zhdanov, *The International Situation* (Moscow: Foreign Languages Publishing House, 1947); and William Z. Foster, *The Meaning of the 9-Party Communist Conference* (New York: New Century Publishers, 1947).

85. "For Lasting Peace for a People's Democracy," Bucharest, March 1 & March 15, 1949.

ABOUT THE AUTHORS

JOSEPH H. ALEXANDER, a retired Colonel in the United States Marine Corps, has written several books and articles on World War II in the Pacific, including *Edson's Raiders: The 1st Marine Raider Battalion in World War II* (Naval Institute Press, 2000) and *Storm Landings: Epic Amphibious Battles in the Central Pacific* (Naval Institute Press, 1997). His many awards include the Samuel Eliot Morison Award from the Naval Order of the United States, the Roosevelt Naval History Prize, and the Alfred Thayer Mahan Award for Literary Achievement. He was the chief historian for twenty-two documentaries for A&E and The History Channel. He has published essays in *Naval Institute Proceedings, Naval History,* and *Marine Corps Gazette,* and was Naval Institute Author of the Year in 1997. Mr. Alexander has degrees in history and government from the University of North Carolina at Chapel Hill, Jacksonville University, and Georgetown University, and is a distinguished graduate of the Naval War College. His Marine Corps duty included two combat tours in Vietnam.

STEPHEN E. AMBROSE is the author of more than twenty books, including *The Wild Blue: The Men and Boys Who Flew the B-24s Over Germany; Citizen Soldiers; Band of Brothers;* and *D-Day: The Climatic Battle of WWII.* He is the retired Boyd Professor of History at the

University of New Orleans, the Director Emeritus of the Eisenhower Center in New Orleans, and the Founder of the National D-Day Museum. He is a contributing editor of the *Quarterly Journal of Military History*, and a director of American Rivers and of the Lewis and Clark Bicentennial Council. His book, *Band of Brothers,* has been made into an HBO mini-series; he was the historical consultant for the movie *Saving Private Ryan*; and he has participated in several television programs produced by The History Channel and by National Geographic. Mr. Ambrose is currently conducting research for a new book, *Citizen Soldiers of the Pacific.*

THOMAS H. CONNER joined the Hillsdale College Faculty in 1983, after completing his Ph.D. in Modern European History at the University of North Carolina at Chapel Hill. His previous and current positions at Hillsdale include Chair of the Department of History, Dean of the Faculty, and Dean of the Division of Social Sciences, and he was voted Hillsdale College Professor of the Year in 1989 and 1999. His scholarly field of specialization is modern French history, and his teaching fields are Western and American Heritage, Russian History, Nineteenth and Twentieth Century European History, and the two World Wars. Dr. Conner regularly leads tours of European battlefields for Hillsdale students, alumni, and friends.

MARTIN GILBERT became the official biographer of Winston Churchill in 1968. Prior to that, he served in the British Army for two years before entering Oxford University in 1957. His many publications include his eight-volume biography of Churchill; his one-volume *Churchill: A Life*; twelve edited volumes of Churchill documents; a series of historical atlases; a three-volume history of the twentieth century; and a work of general history on the Holocaust. His film and television work includes the script for the Academy Award-winning film *Genocide*; the three-hour Masterpiece Theatre dramatization of his book, *Churchill, The Wilderness Years;* and three recent films for The History Channel on the Kovno ghetto, the Israeli War of Independence, and Jerusalem. He has lectured widely, including at the Ukrainian Academy of Sciences in Kiev, the Ministry of Defense in Moscow, and the State Department in Washington, D.C. Mr. Gilbert was knighted, becoming Sir Martin, in 1995.

VICTOR DAVIS HANSON, a professor of classics at California State University, Fresno, received his B.A. in classics at the University of California at Santa Cruz and his Ph.D. in classics from Stanford University. In 1991 he was given the Award for Teaching Excellence by the American Philological Association—an annual citation given to the top undergraduate teachers of classics. He is the author or editor of several books on military and ancient history, including *The Wars of the Ancient Greeks* (Cassell, 1999), *The Soul of Battle* (The Free Press, 1999), and *Carnage and Culture* (Doubleday, 2001). His books have been History Club and Book of the Month Club selections, and have been translated into Italian, Spanish, German, French, and Greek. His articles and reviews have appeared in *The Wall Street Journal,* the *New York Times,* the *Washington Times, American Heritage, The Weekly Standard,* and *The Wilson Quarterly,* and he has been featured on National Public Radio and the *Jim Lehrer News Hour.* Dr. Hanson lives with his wife and three children on the farm where he was born in Selma, California.

FREDERICK W. KAGAN is an associate professor of military history at the United States Military Academy at West Point. His books include *While America Sleeps: Self-Delusion, Military Weakness and the Threat to Peace Today* (St. Martin's, 2000), co-authored with Donald Kagan, and *The Military Reforms of Nicholas I: The Origins of the Modern Russian Army* (Palgrave, 1999). He has written and spoken extensively on current American strategy and military policy, and published articles in *The Wall Street Journal, Commentary, The Weekly Standard,* and *Parameters*. He is currently writing the first of three volumes in a history of the wars between Napoleon and Russia.

JOHN LUKACS is emeritus professor of history at Chestnut Hill College. Born in Hungary, he came to the United States in 1946. He holds a diploma from Cambridge University and a degree from Budapest University. His many teaching posts include La Salle College, the University of Pennsylvania, the University of Toulouse, and the University of Budapest. He is the recipient of several academic honors and awards, including the Ingersoll Prize, and is the author of countless books, including *The Hitler of History* (Knopf, 1997); *Five Days in London, May 1940* (Yale, 1999); *George F. Kennan and the Origins of Containment, 1944–46: The Kennan–Lukacs Correspondence* (University of Missouri, 1997); and *The End of the Twentieth Century and The End of the Modern Age* (Hougton Mifflin, 1993), which was nominated for the Pulitzer Prize. Dr. Lukacs was awarded the Cross of Merit by the Republic of Hungary in 1994, and lives with his wife in Pennsylvania.

HERBERT ROMERSTEIN retired in 1989 as head of the Office to Counter Soviet Disinformation and Active Measures at the United States Information Agency. Prior to that he was a professional staff member for the United States House of Representatives, where he served as Investigator for the House Committee on Un-American Activities (1965–1971); Minority Chief Investigator for the House Committee on Internal Security (1971–1975); and on the staff of the House Intelligence Committee (1978–1983). His many Congressional Reports, books, monographs, and articles include *The Venona Secrets: Exposing Soviet Espionage and America's Traitors* (Regnery, 2000), co-authored with the late Eric Breindel, which is based on Soviet intelligence communication intercepted by the United States, Congressional Hearings and Reports, FBI material released under the Freedom of Information Act, and documents that Mr. Romerstein and his wife obtained in Moscow from the Soviet Archives.

GERHARD L. WEINBERG is the Emeritus William Rand Kenan Jr. Professor of History at the University of North Carolina at Chapel Hill. His numerous awards include the Guggenheim Fellowship; the National Endowment for the Humanities Fellowship; the 1971 George Louis Beer Prize of the American Historical Association for his book, *The Foreign Policy of Hitler's Germany, 1933–1936*; and the 1995 Herbert Hoover Presidential Library Association award for his book, *A World at Arms: A Global History of World War II*. He has been a member of The American Academy of Arts and Sciences since 1996; he serves on the Board of Directors of the World War II Studies Association; he is a former member of the Board of Editors of *The International History Review*; and he served as Consultant to the United States Holocaust Memorial Council in 1992. Dr. Weinberg currently chairs the United States Army Historical Advisory Committee and the Advisory Panel of the Interagency Working Group implementing the Nazi War Crimes Disclosure Act, and is a member of the U.S. Army Training and Doctrine Command Military History Council.